GW00758844

1 CHEEK
2 NECK
3 SHOULDER
4 BACK FAT
5 LOIN
6 RIBS
7 BELLY
8 LEG

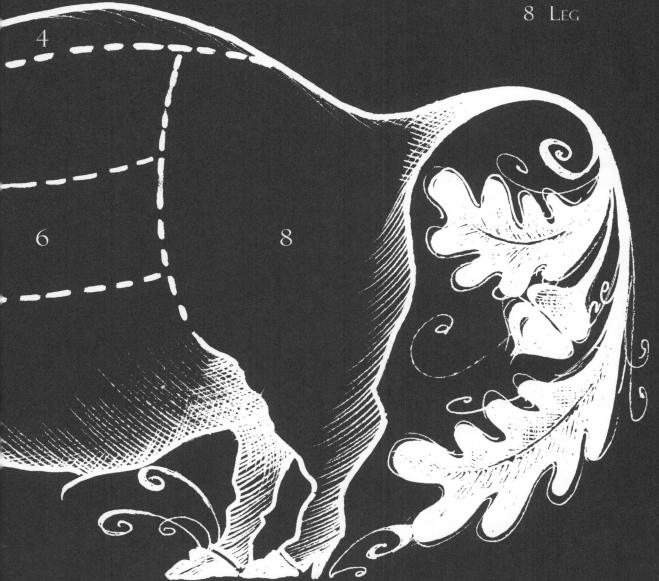

SALT YARD

RECIPES BY BEN TISH

First published in Great Britain in 2012
Published by Piquillo Publishing
Salt Yard, 54 Goodge Street, London, W1T 4NA

Text © Ben Tish, Sanja Morris and Simon Mullins 2012
Photography © Jason Lowe 2012

The rights of the authors have been asserted.
All rights reserved. No part of this work may be reproduced or utilised in any
form or by any means, electronic or mechanical, including photocopying,
recording or by any information storage and retrieval system, without the
prior written permission of the publishers.

A catalogue record of this book is available from the British Library.

ISBN 978-0-9573630-0-7

RECIPES: Ben Tish
PROJECT CO-ORDINATION: Sanja Morris
WINE: Simon Mullins
DESIGN: Helen Driver www.helendriver.co.uk
DESIGN CONSULTANT: David Driver
PHOTOGRAPHY: Jason Lowe
COVER & ENDPAPER ILLUSTRATIONS: Pedro D'Almeida
EDITOR: Priscilla Morris
ILLUSTRATIONS: Ramon Otting (pages 12, 40, 60, 86,122,154)
ILLUSTRATIONS: David Driver (pages 14, 42, 62,156)
ILLUSTRATIONS: reproduced with the kind permission of Louise Body
www.louisebody.com (pages 11, 39, 58, 59, 193)
CONTRIBUTIONS: Stephen Bayley, Kevin Gould, Max Halley
RECIPE CONTRIBUTIONS: Andrew Clarke, Jamie Thickett, Giancarlo Vatteroni

Printed in England by Pureprint Group, Uckfield, on Arctic Volume Paper, an FSC ® certified grade.
Typesetting in Monotype Grotesque. Headlines in Felix Titling.

SALT YARD

FOOD & WINE
FROM SPAIN & ITALY

PHOTOGRAPHS BY JASON LOWE
PROJECT CO-ORDINATOR SANJA MORRIS

SANJA MORRIS   BEN TISH   SIMON MULLINS

PIQUILLO PUBLISHING FITZROVIA LONDON

CONTENTS

HOW IT ALL BEGAN

By Sanja Morris

Salt Yard was a defunct sushi restaurant when we took it over. The owner had left, seemingly mid-service, a few weeks before and when we went into the kitchen, we gagged on the smell of tray after tray of rotting fish. The place was characterised by piles: piles of dirty crockery, piles of stained cushions, piles of half-used cleaning products, and one particularly memorable pile, which was made up of a mangled deep fat fryer, several stainless steel shelves, a pair of old curtains and a dozen or so mousetraps. It was not promising.

Our families and friends came to help. We cleared, cleaned, bleached and scrubbed. My mother loved it. We filled a skip out the back and watched through the window as every tramp in Fitzrovia descended onto the rubbish in the bleak January snow and cleared the lot. Where were they going with five hundred sachets of soy sauce? With torn-open, five-kilogram bags of flour? With a broken toilet seat? The walls were painted a deep burgundy; bar stools from a millionaire's yacht were bought on eBay and collected in Knightsbridge; rise and fall ceiling lights from France were fitted. We went to Snappy Snaps to blow up photos we'd taken ourselves in Spain and hung them on the freshly-painted walls. Habitat shelves were altered and put up behind the bar to hold the wine. We typed, laminated and stapled our menus. And finally, a grand booking system was devised which consisted of a Ryman's diary and a pencil. In short, it was done on a shoestring.

However, the real work started much earlier – with eating and drinking, of course. Eating and drinking in every small restaurant in New York. Eating and drinking our way round Barcelona, Valencia and San Sebastian. Eating and drinking in every trattoria and bar in Venice, Bologna and Rome. That was the heart of our work. And so it was with setting up the restaurant, too. Once the necessary dullness of talking to our bank manager, our solicitor, the drain man, the electrician, and so on was out of the way, we sat down amongst the piles and...started to eat and drink. Brian, our head chef, brought dish after dish from the kitchen – crisp, earthy morcilla croquetas, sticky ribs marinated in Pedro Ximénez, deep-fried baby artichokes – all for us to taste and accept or reject. Suppliers came over with dozens of cheeses with names we had never heard of, and hams which we still have on the menu today. Our friends dropped by after work and tried wine after wine telling us what they wanted in a house red or white and what sort of fizz they liked. We took illegible notes.

Then, in the blink of an eye, Salt Yard was open. And it was good. And busy, really busy. People were everywhere, eating, drinking and chatting. They were sitting at the bar, drinking cold sherry with a plate of freshly carved Jamón Ibérico, like we had done in Valencia; sitting outside with a glass of prosecco and some marinated sardines, as we had done in Venice; while at romantic Table 15 at the back of the restaurant, they were leaning in close over a plate of five cheeses with honey and large glasses of Barolo.

Two years later, Ben Tish joined us as executive chef and the three of us decided to do it again – and then, another two years later, a third time. Dehesa was a decades-old greasy spoon in Soho with three feet of fake ceiling and an expanse of Formica floor. Opera Tavern was a faded pub near the Opera House in Covent Garden, solidly built but with asbestos in the basement. With rather more professional help second and third time round, we transformed them and made places where we, and everyone we know, love to eat and drink.

Cooking, choosing the wine, setting the table and meeting your guests' needs are all acts of creation and hospitality. When we set up Salt Yard we wanted to create that sense of hospitality in a city which for some reason had only a handful of good restaurants actually serving good food at good prices. For the most part, restaurants in London seemed to be intent on taking as much of people's money as possible and, in exchange, giving them the lowest quality food served by the most harassed waiters. London has now blossomed. Soho, Fitzrovia, Smithfield and Bermondsey heave with small, independent restaurants which all have the same goal: proper hospitality. The word derives from the Latin 'hospes' which is thought to be formed from two separate roots: 'hostis', meaning 'stranger or guest' and 'potis', meaning 'power'. A good restaurant doesn't abuse its power over its guests. It honours it.

Hospitality is enjoyable because it's an active way of showing you care about someone. Making Sunday lunch for ten people or a five-course meal for your partner are ways of showing you love them, him or her. Thumbing through a cookbook, going to the shops, finding special ingredients, marinating a piece of meat overnight, chopping vegetables in the late morning with a glass of wine, filling your kitchen with the smell of unusual spices, trying out a pudding which is slightly more complicated than you're used to, cutting a few flowers from your battered city rose bush to put on the table and then forgetting to serve the handmade condiment with your cheeses – it's all done to please other people and make them happy in a way which doesn't need words.

The recipes in this cookbook are, of course, all written with words. But they're a means to help you recreate in your home some of the sunshine of the Mediterranean and the hospitality and joy of a good restaurant. Follow them word for word or simply use them as inspiration. As with setting up a restaurant, there's no precise formula for creating something good. Just use top quality ingredients, invite your favourite people over, relax, open a bottle of wine and enjoy!

Sanja Morris co-founded Salt Yard in 2005, Dehesa in 2008 and Opera Tavern in 2011 with Simon Mullins. Prior to that she worked for the British Council, promoting UK creative industries abroad.

Simon Mullins co-founded the Salt Yard Group restaurants with Sanja. Previously, he worked for Spanish food importer Brindisa and before that he worked in advertising.

Ben Tish joined Salt Yard in 2006 as executive chef and set up Dehesa and Opera Tavern with Sanja and Simon. Before joining, he honed his craft at the Ritz, Coast, the Crinan Hotel and Al Duca.

From left Ben Tish, Sanja Morris and Simon Mullins

FOOD NOTES

The dishes served in our restaurants are designed for sharing. For ease, the recipes here have been designed for 4 people as a first or main course and for 6–8 people as a tapa.

- All temperatures given in the recipes are for conventional ovens. Decrease by 10–20°C for fan-assisted ovens.
- Large, free-range or organic eggs are called for in these recipes.
- Salt should be Maldon sea salt.
- Sugar is caster, unless otherwise stated.

WINE NOTES

We're as passionate about wine as we are about food. We believe the best way to demystify and enjoy wine is to have fun and experiment with it.

Every fish, meat, vegetable and pudding recipe in this book has a wine match, suggesting the perfect grape type and region to partner your food. When it comes to bar snacks and charcuterie, a glass of bubbles is always a good way to start the meal! Prosecco and cava are both delicious, generally cheaper alternatives to champagne.

To enjoy the wines we've recommended, ditch the supermarket and track down a good local independent wine shop instead. Go exploring, armed with some of our suggestions. Any decent wine shop should know the wines we've mentioned, so all you have to do is ask. To give you a head start, we've compiled a small list of wine shops and websites at the back of this book where you're likely to find the wines we've suggested. So, happy hunting – and happy supping!

FROM SMALL ACORNS DO MIGHTY HAMS GROW

BY KEVIN GOULD

Kevin Gould is a food and wine writer. He has hosted wine events at Dehesa.

This is the tale of a few beautiful Autumn days when Ben Tish and I journeyed with Brindisa, the master supplier of Spanish ingredients, in search of the ultimate Ibérico ham for Salt Yard's restaurants...

Miguel González looks like a Spanish Lee Marvin. We're somewhere near Salamanca, strolling the dehesa of his pig farm, which smells of warm earth and wild herbs. The pure Ibérico or pata negra pig is an impressive beast. Straight of back, lean of flank, well-muscled, but with the daintiest of ankles, this pedigree pig has a noble bloodline stretching back thousands of years. The González herd is more semi-wild than free-range as Miguel/Lee allows only one pig per three hectares of dehesa. We see a few of them gambolling in contented, dusty groups, truffling for fallen acorns, roots and grasses. Larks, swifts and golden orioles call to each other across this ancient tree-studded pastureland, which is dotted with encina (holm oak, *Quercus ilex*) trees. To an Ibérico pig the encina's acorns are haute cuisine, fine wine and great chocolate in one neat nibble. It's the acorn's oleic-rich oils and sweet proteins that make real Ibérico meat so healthy and delectable.

Guijuelo is central Spain's Pig Central. It is also pig ugly. The town's houses are drab and plain and its streets are built to no apparent plan — even the bars have a square, functional air. But to the ham aficionado, Guijuelo's air is heaven, with its constant, clean, gentle winds and a climate that's never too hot, too cold or too humid.

Down an anonymous road are the premises of Castro y González, master curers and maturers of Ibérico ham. Maestro Miguel tells us that taken together, purity of breed, quality of feed and age, create the exceptional ham. Purity means DNA testing and DOC certification. By quality of feed, he means mother's milk, then grains, then great snoutfuls of sweet acorns. Age is about more than just the 20 months it takes for a pig to grow: Sr. González's notion of time includes the generations that his family have spent breeding and slow-growing Ibérico pigs, and the millions of hours they've spent curing and maturing their hams.

First, a tour of the salting rooms, where the hams and shoulders are cured in crunchy crystals of sea salt from Isla Cristina; one day of salting per kilo of meat. Because each joint weighs differently, each joint receives individual personal attention from Aurélio, Miguel's second son. The rooms smell marvellously yeasty and are maintained at 20°C and 100% humidity. Each day scores of joints leave the salting rooms, having been miraculously cured. They are borne upstairs to the darkened maturing rooms, where pretty, plaited cords are tied around each pert ankle and the hams and shoulders are hung together, hip-to-toe, five-high, in dense, silent forests of ham. The maturing floors are amazing. In this cloistered hush, tens of thousands of hams are slowly, splendidly evolving. They're hung in long arcades and avenues, in side rooms and around corners, above your head, and at eye level too. As with curing, each ham receives individual care. They are massaged with olive oil or tocino (rendered Ibérico fat) to encourage the flowering of beneficial yeasts that will protect the hams during their long sojourn here. The hams produce rich, sweet, healthy, meaty aromas that make us ravenously hungry.

A cala is like a darning needle fashioned from a horse's hip bone. By pushing the cala into various parts of a ham, then sniffing it, Miguel the Master Maturer understands how each ham is developing. Should it be moved up to a livelier floor where the air circulates more freely, or to a quiet side room for a few weeks' rest from the crowd? Air circulation is managed by simply opening windows on one or the other side of the building. These windows are covered with beautiful blinds woven from esparto grass. Through these blinds enters a marvellously diffused light, which lends the maturing rooms the atmosphere of a cathedral. A high priest of his art, Miguel González has the raw material, technique and experience to mature his hams for as long as five years. This unusually lengthy ageing amplifies their Guijuelo character – a tender, elegant texture that's juicy in the mouth, bursting with complex, natural sweetness. Ben and I confirm

this for ourselves via an intensive tasting session. In truth, this is less a scientific, scholarly exercise and more the chance to make honking pigs of ourselves. The absolute favourite is Miguel's five-year riserva. Here my notes grow hysterical with the sheer indulgent luxury of it all, observing how, 'each sexy chew contains the very essence of deep savouriness,' and that, 'this is how rubies and velvet would taste, if they were food – and you were eating them to the sound of birdsong and flamenco.' Time for a lie down.

The lowdown on these Ibérico hams is that they are one of the world's greatest hand-made luxury foods. Their production is born of a rare pact between nature and humans, beast and feed, terroir and technique, plus that extra something – the special magic that transforms these hams from the merely excellent into the absolutely sublime. This magic ingredient? Let's just say that tasting one of these hams helps connect you with something of the timeless, mysterious spirit of Spain's vast heart. This Ibérico ham is food for the soul, food to lift your mood, and proof that from small acorns do mighty hams grow.

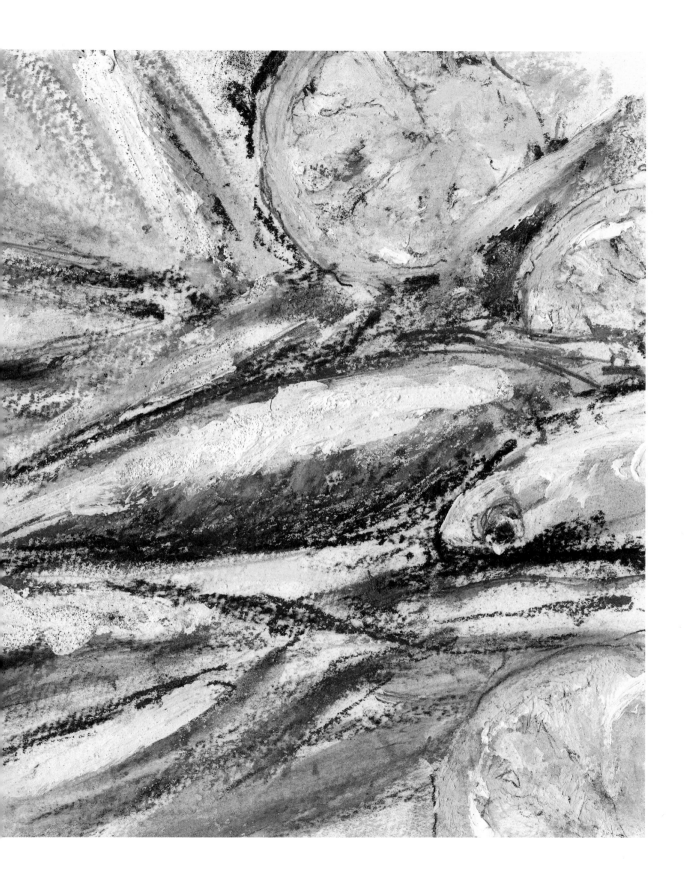

NIBBLES

The general idea behind our nibbles is that they're small enough to be picked up with one hand, while the other is left free for the serious business of drinking and gesticulating, as they love to do in Spanish and Italian bars. Our snacks are served throughout the day at the restaurants. They're great for customers who fancy a small bite and a little glass of something in the afternoon, or as a pre-meal nibble to get the appetite going in the evening. Bar snacks range from the extremely simple, buttery Marcona almonds, spicy guindilla peppers and fresh, bright green Nocellara del Belice olives, to those requiring more preparation, such as grilled pinchos morunos, rich duck liver and sherry paté, courgette fries with tomato alioli and our crispy Ibérico pigs' ears.

We've even developed our own take on the British pub classic, the Scotch egg. Ramping up the flavour with marjoram and adding a dollop of alioli as a dipping sauce has made it a firm favourite on our bar snack menu.

The culture of enjoying a snack whilst drinking hasn't developed much in the UK beyond peanuts, crisps and pork scratchings – most Britons go to the pub to drink, and all else is secondary. But in Spain and Italy, it's the combined experience of eating, drinking and socialising that counts and it's rare to find a bar that doesn't offer a selection of toothsome nibbles to accompany your aperitif. Walk into any bar in Venice and you'll find an array of tasty bar snacks and cicchetti to accompany your glass of prosecco or Negroni. Cicchetti are Italian-style tapas that focus heavily on raw and cured fish and often have citrus dressings. Bite-sized crostini spread with salt cod brandade or piled high with pickled vegetables and chopped spicy olives are also popular. Italians love fried nibbles, so you may also find crispy squid or deep-fried, breaded olives stuffed with meat served alongside your drink.

In Spain, besides the popular plates of hot, salty Padrón peppers, tins of fish and vegetables are commonly opened to order to go with your cerveza, Txacoli or light sherry – and are eaten standing at the bar. Unlike here, these tinned products are taken very seriously and are of extremely high standard – at times constituting the bar's sole food offering. There certainly couldn't be a simpler snack if time is short and we've elaborated on this with our smoked anchovy recipe in this section.

When deciding on which nibbles to serve, remember: nothing too subtle or bland. Bar snacks should be full-flavoured and spicy or salty so they'll stimulate the taste buds in preparation for the meal, or tapas, to come. The recipes given here are designed with that in mind. On the whole they're quick to prepare, often requiring little more than the assembly of one or two ingredients – which means you've got more time to enjoy drinking and socialising with your guests.

PADRÓN PEPPERS

A tapas feast just wouldn't be complete without a serving of hot, salty Padrón peppers. It's said that about one in ten of the little green peppers is rocket fuel, so sharing a plate can be a bit like a game of Russian roulette! Padrón peppers are available in most of the larger supermarkets now, so do give them a try. Make sure you use Maldon sea salt flakes – there's simply no alternative.

Serves 4

200g Padrón peppers

olive oil for cooking

sea salt

Heat a large sauté pan over a high heat. When the pan is hot, add a good lug of olive oil and then tip in the Padrón peppers. If your pan isn't big enough to fit in all the peppers comfortably, you will need to fry in 2 batches.

Cook the peppers until they start to brown and blister, and then turn over – or toss, if confident – to cook their undersides. Padrón peppers cook quickly and shouldn't take longer than 5 minutes – though if they are still firm to the touch after this time, they will need a little more time in the pan.

When done, transfer the peppers to kitchen paper to drain and sprinkle liberally with sea salt. Serve piping hot.

QUAIL'S EGGS

WITH PAPRIKA SALT

This is a hugely popular bar snack at our restaurants, which was originally inspired by the classic British combination of gull's eggs and celery salt. Quail's eggs are the perfect size for a nibble and are now readily available in most places. Make sure you buy a good-quality sweet smoked paprika to mix with the salt: it will make all the difference. The paprika salt is a great condiment to have in the store cupboard, so make a larger batch, if you like, and keep in a sealed jar.

Serves 4

12 quail's eggs

1 tablespoon good-quality sweet smoked paprika

2 tablespoons sea salt

Bring a small pan of salted water to the boil. Carefully lower in the eggs and cook for 3 minutes. When cooked, run cold water into the pan to cool the eggs.

Peel the top half of the eggs and leave the bottom half intact for attractive presentation.

Mix the paprika and sea salt together, transfer to a shallow dish and serve alongside the half-peeled eggs. Your guests can peel and dip the eggs into the paprika salt as they eat.

Italian-Style Scotch Egg

When we set up Opera Tavern, we wanted to give a nod to its public house heritage and so added a few pub classics to the menu, each with our own distinctive Spanish-Italian twist. These Scotch eggs are given some Italian flavours with the use of pork and veal mince, mixed with marjoram and lemon zest. Cook the eggs just before they're to be eaten, so they're hot and crisp on the outside and the yolk is warm and runny in the middle. They're delicious dipped in some homemade alioli and washed down with a glass of cold beer.

Makes 6 scotch eggs

6 medium free-range or organic eggs

180g minced British rose veal

180g minced pork

zest of 1 lemon

2 teaspoons marjoram leaves

plain flour, sifted, enough for coating the eggs

5 eggs, beaten

panko-style breadcrumbs, enough for coating the eggs

2 litres vegetable oil for deep-frying

alioli (optional), for dipping the eggs in (see Basics)

sea salt and black pepper

Bring a pan of water to a rolling boil, carefully lower the eggs into the water and cook for about 6½ minutes. Remove and place in a bowl of iced water. Leave for 5 minutes or so until completely cool. Very carefully peel the eggs.

Place both the minces and the lemon zest in a mixing bowl. Roughly chop half the marjoram and add to the mince mixture. Season lightly and mix thoroughly. You can test a small piece of the mince by frying it in olive oil until cooked through: taste to see if you're happy with the flavouring and seasoning, and adjust as necessary.

Divide the mince mixture into 6 equal pieces. Flatten one piece on a lightly oiled chopping board to make an oval shape about 3mm thick. Sit an egg on top and wrap the mince around it, ensuring there are no air gaps between the egg and the mince and that the mince is distributed evenly. Be very gentle so you don't break the egg, which is still runny inside. Repeat with the other eggs.

Place the flour, beaten eggs and breadcrumbs in 3 separate bowls. Roll each egg first in the flour, then in the egg and finally in the breadcrumbs. Make sure you coat the egg evenly at each stage. When all the eggs are breaded, coat them once more in the egg and again in the breadcrumbs (but not the flour this time). This second coating is the secret behind a wonderfully crispy crust. If the breadcrumbs become too gooey and clumped together, use another bowl of fresh breadcrumbs. It's important that you have a nice, light coating.

Heat the oil in a tall-sided pan until a piece of bread fizzles and browns when dropped in, or heat the oil in a deep fat fryer to 170°C.

Lower 3 eggs into the oil and fry until golden brown, which should take about 4 minutes. Turn the eggs while they fry to colour evenly on all sides. Transfer the eggs to some kitchen paper and repeat the procedure with the remaining eggs. When done, transfer to a baking tray and place in a warm oven for 3 minutes to further heat through.

Slice the eggs in half lengthwise and sprinkle with sea salt and pepper. Serve strewn with fresh marjoram leaves and the alioli on the side, if you like.

CRESCENTINE

WITH BROAD BEANS & SMOKED RICOTTA

Crescentina is a type of fried flatbread which hails from Emilia-Romagna in Italy. Italian crescentine are typically much larger than ours and have pork lard folded through the dough, which is delicious. We have adapted the classic recipe slightly by making them into bite-size flatbreads, perfect for a snack or nibble, and replacing the pork lard with extra virgin olive oil. Sweet broad beans, at their best in the summer months, are paired here with smoked ricotta. Regular ricotta will work fine too.

Serves 4–6

For the crescentine dough:

1 heaped teaspoon dried yeast, or

2 teaspoons fresh yeast

60ml tepid full cream milk

125g plain flour, sifted

a pinch of table salt

1 tablespoon extra virgin olive oil

olive oil for cooking

For the topping:

180g peeled broad beans, fresh or frozen

120g smoked or regular ricotta, crumbled into small chunks

3 tablespoons extra virgin olive oil

juice of 1 lemon

zest of ½ lemon

8 mint leaves, roughly chopped

sea salt and black pepper

Activate the yeast by pouring it into the tepid milk. Mix together the flour, salt and olive oil in a large mixing bowl. Slowly stir in the milk and yeast to form a dough. Mix the dough for 2 minutes or so and then leave in the bowl to prove for about 1 hour or until it has doubled in size.

Place the dough on a floured surface and 'knock back' or knead well to push out any air. Roll the dough to a thickness of about 2mm, adding more flour as necessary to prevent the dough sticking to the surface. Cut out circles of dough with a 5cm-diameter pastry cutter and transfer to a large, well-floured plate.

Heat a large sauté pan over a medium heat and pour about 1cm of olive oil into the pan for shallow-frying the bread. When the oil is hot and a piece of dough fizzles on contact, cook the discs of dough in batches until they are golden brown and start to puff up. Transfer the bread to kitchen paper, once cooked.

To make the topping, either use the broad beans raw, if very tender, or cook in salted, boiling water for a couple of minutes. Mix the beans together with all the other topping ingredients in a bowl and season to taste. Spoon the ricotta and bean mixture equally over the crescentine and serve.

COURGETTE FRIES
WITH TOMATO ALIOLI

An interesting alternative to French fries. These courgette fries are often found in Venetian cicchetti bars and we have paired them here with a tangy, sweet tomato alioli which is very simple to make. If you have a mandoline with a 'spaghetti' cutter attachment, this will make light work of slicing the courgettes – otherwise a sharp knife will do. Depending on taste, you can sprinkle the fries with chopped fresh thyme or rosemary leaves as soon as they come out of the oil.

Serves 4–6

For the fries:

4 large courgettes, ends trimmed

2 litres olive oil for deep-frying

milk for dipping

plain flour for dredging

sea salt and black pepper

For the tomato alioli:

100g ripe cherry tomatoes, cut in half

a pinch of caster sugar

1 teaspoon Cabernet Sauvignon vinegar or other red wine vinegar

olive oil

200ml alioli (see Basics)

fresh thyme or rosemary, chopped (optional)

First, the tomato alioli. Place the tomatoes in a small saucepan with the sugar, vinegar and a splash of olive oil. Season with salt. Place the pan on a high heat and crush the tomatoes with the back of a fork to break them down a bit. Turn the heat to low and cook the tomatoes for about 30 minutes, crushing at regular intervals with the fork. Aim to reduce the tomatoes to a rough, dryish paste. Allow the paste to cool and then stir through the alioli.

Using a mandoline or a sharp knife, slice the courgettes very thinly lengthwise, and then slice each length into thin strips. You want to achieve long French fries. Place the courgette chips in a colander and sprinkle with sea salt. Put the colander over a bowl and leave for 20 minutes, allowing the salt to draw out the excess moisture from the courgettes. Pat the courgettes dry with kitchen paper.

Heat the olive oil to 170°C in a deep fat fryer, or until a courgette chip fizzles when dropped into a deep-sided saucepan. Place the milk and flour in separate bowls. Dip the courgette pieces first in the milk and then dredge in the flour. Carefully lower half the fries into the oil and move them around with a spatula to ensure they colour evenly. When golden brown and crisp, drain on kitchen paper. Repeat with the second batch. Sprinkle with Maldon sea salt and chopped herbs, if desired. Transfer to serving bowls and serve with the alioli on the side.

GRILLED BOCCONCINI DI CAPRA
WITH PLUMS

Grilled goat's cheese became fashionable in the 1960s, so this is quite a retro choice but delicious nonetheless. Bocconcini di Capra is an Italian goat's cheese from Piedmont and is wonderful lightly grilled. If you can't find it, a good substitute would be any soft goat's cheese from the UK or France. Just make sure it has a good rind to hold its shape when it's grilled. The lovely plums are a great foil to the rich goat's cheese – and can be used as a condiment for most other cheeses as well.

Serves 4

150g Bocconcini di Capra or other goat's cheese, sliced into 4 even rounds

3 small plums, halved, stones removed

25g caster sugar

1 tablespoon Moscatel vinegar or white balsamic vinegar

1 sprig thyme

sea salt and black pepper

Slice the plums into even pieces and place in a small saucepan with the sugar, vinegar and thyme over a medium heat. Cook the plums for 20–25 minutes, occasionally stirring, until the plums have broken down into a rich, jammy consistency. Season with salt and pepper and reserve.

Heat the grill to maximum heat. Lay a sheet of baking paper on the grill pan and place the rounds of cheese on top. Put the pan under the grill until the cheese is lightly browned and just starting to bubble. Remove the cheese from the grill, season with black pepper and then carefully transfer to a plate with a spatula. Serve with some sourdough bread and the plum jam.

SMOKED EEL BRANDADE

Eels have long been on the unsustainable list, but it's recently become possible to choose eels that have come from rivers which are continuously restocked with baby eels to replace the ones caught. Just ask your fishmonger. This is great news for chefs and foodies, allowing us to eat the delicious, traditional English river fish guilt-free. If you can't find eel, a good-quality smoked mackerel will do. Try serving this rich brandade with some hot, buttered sourdough toast and a poached egg for breakfast. Delicious.

Serves 4

200g sustainable smoked eel fillets

500ml full cream milk

100ml double cream

2 cloves garlic, unpeeled and crushed

2 medium Désirée potatoes, peeled and diced

2 tablespoons flat-leaf parsley, chopped

juice of ½ lemon

sea salt and black pepper

Place the milk and cream in a medium-sized saucepan over a low heat. Add the eel and garlic and bring slowly to the boil. Simmer for 2 minutes to allow the milk to infuse with the smokiness of the eel. Carefully remove the eel from the milk and reserve.

Add the potatoes to the smoky milk and cook over a low heat until they are soft and tender. When cooked, remove the potatoes from the milk and add them to the bowl with the eel. Continue to cook the milk, reducing it down by about a third until quite thick and syrupy. Turn off the heat and discard the garlic.

Lightly crush the potatoes and eel together with a fork to form a rough paste and then slowly add the reduced milk, followed by the chopped parsley and lemon juice. Mix everything together and season if necessary. Serve in ramekins with sourdough bread or toast.

SMOKED ANCHOVIES

WITH BUTTER, SHALLOT & PARSLEY SALAD

The tinned anchovy is ubiquitous in tapas bars and restaurants all over Spain. The Spanish take the little fish very seriously indeed and consider it a real delicacy. Certain premium brands, such as Ortiz and Nardin, which promise the highest quality fish are revered throughout the country. But in the UK, the anchovy, on the whole, is considered a second-rate fish: flavouring to liven up a bland dish at best. Get your hands on some imported Spanish beauties, now stocked in most larger supermarkets and delis, and you'll never underestimate the little fellow again.

Serves 4

100g tin smoked anchovies

1 banana shallot, peeled, finely sliced into rings

a generous handful of flat-leaf parsley leaves

½ lemon for squeezing

a few slices of toasted bread of your choice (we like ciabatta, sliced thinly and toasted, with salt and olive oil)

60g unsalted butter at room temperature

sea salt and black pepper

This recipe is exceedingly simple. Open the tin and divide the anchovies between individual serving plates or transfer to one large plate, as you prefer. Serving the anchovies at room temperature will ensure the fullest flavour.

Put the shallots and parsley in a bowl, season with salt and pepper, and add a good squeeze of lemon juice and a little of the oil from the anchovy tin.

Mix the shallot and parsley salad and serve with the anchovies, the toasted bread and the butter. Eat all together: the salad on top of the anchovies on top of the hot, buttered toast. Enjoy!

Venetian-Style Sardines

A classic Venetian cicchetti: the Italian version of tapas and largely based around fresh and cured fish. The strong flavour of sardine works wonders against the sweet-sour back drop of the pickled onions and raisins. The toasted pine nuts finish and add textural contrast to the dish. Try using mackerel fillets or herring if you can't find the sardines.

Serves 4

8 sardine fillets

1 large Spanish onion, peeled, finely sliced

1 clove garlic, finely chopped

2 bay leaves

1 tablespoon demerara sugar

1 tablespoon raisins

2 tablespoons Moscatel vinegar or white balsamic vinegar

1 tablespoon pine nuts

1 tablespoon flat-leaf parsley, chopped

a squeeze of lemon

olive oil for cooking

sea salt and black pepper

Preheat the grill to 160°C.

Set a saucepan over a medium heat and add a good lug of olive oil. Throw in the onions, garlic and bay leaves and coat well in the oil. Season well and cook for 30 minutes until soft and tender but without too much colour. Sprinkle in the sugar and add the vinegar and the raisins. Continue to cook for a further 20 minutes. Lightly toast the pine nuts under the grill until light brown and add to the onions. Turn off the heat and let the onions rest.

Season the sardine fillets on both sides and sprinkle with olive oil. Place skin-side up on a non-stick tray and grill briefly for around 2 minutes. The sardines should be partially cooked and the skin slightly browned. Transfer some of the onions to a large dish and then layer the sardines on top followed by the remaining onions. Transfer to the fridge and leave to marinate for at least 3 hours.

Take the sardines and onions out of the fridge and allow them to come up to room temperature before serving. Scatter with some chopped flat-leaf parsley and add a squeeze of lemon. Some ciabatta crostini sprinkled with olive oil would go very well here.

EMPANADILLAS

Originating in Galicia and Portugal, these small stuffed pastries first sprang up in the Iberian Peninsula during the time of the Moorish occupation. Versions are to be found all over the world: the calzone is Italy's, the pasty is Britain's and the samosa is India's. We fill ours with whatever is in season at the time. They are a great way of using up any leftover bits of meat or fish. No need to make your own puff pastry: shop-bought is usually excellent quality nowadays and saves time.

Makes 12 empanadillas

400g good-quality, shop-bought
puff pastry

plain flour for dusting

1 egg, beaten, to be used as
egg wash

filling of your choice (page 32)

Preheat the oven to 180°C.

Sprinkle some flour on a clean work surface and roll out the pastry to a 3mm thickness. Cut out discs from the pastry about 12cm in diameter and transfer onto a floured tray. Repeat the process with the leftover pastry: you should end up with 12 discs of pastry. Transfer to the fridge to chill.

Prepare the filling of your choice.

When the pastry has chilled, remove from the fridge and place a heaped teaspoon of filling in the centre of each disc, leaving a 2cm border around the edges. Brush some egg wash on one half of the border and pull the other half over the top of the filling to meet the eggy side. Press down and seal the pastry, ensuring there are no gaps. You will have a half moon shape with a bulge of filling in the centre. The pastry is quite robust but will become warm with too much handling, so you should work fairly swiftly. Crimp the sealed edge with a fork to give the classic empanadilla finish. Brush all over with egg wash and pop in the fridge for at least 15 minutes.

Bake the empanadillas on a floured, non-stick oven tray for 15–20 minutes until the pastry is golden brown and the filling is piping hot – a knife inserted into the centre of the empanadilla will come out hot. Serve immediately.

Empanadillas

Cumin & Paprika-Spiced Chicken & Spinach

120g shredded cooked chicken meat

50g baby spinach leaves

1 teaspoon sweet smoked paprika

½ teaspoon ground cumin

1 teaspoon flat-leaf parsley, chopped

a squeeze of lemon juice

olive oil for cooking

sea salt and black pepper

Heat a sauté pan over a low heat and add a lug of olive oil. Add the paprika and cumin and cook gently for 1 minute. Add the spinach, season, and cook until fully wilted. Drain the spinach, cool and roughly chop. Mix with the chicken, parsley and lemon. Proceed as on page 30.

Crab, Chilli, Lemon & Mint

140g fresh white crabmeat, picked

50g fresh brown crabmeat

1 small red chilli, deseeded, finely chopped

8 mint leaves, finely shredded

juice and zest of ½ lemon

sea salt and black pepper

Sit the brown crabmeat in a sieve for 20 minutes to drain off any excess liquid. Place the white crabmeat in a bowl and mix in the brown crabmeat. Stir in the chilli, mint leaves, lemon zest and juice. Season. Transfer to the fridge to chill for 20 minutes before use. Proceed as on page 30.

Pork, Lemon Thyme, Raisins & Pine Nuts

120g cooked, leftover pork with fat (pork belly is best or use shoulder)

40g raisins, soaked in water for 10 minutes, then drained and finely chopped

2 sprigs lemon thyme, leaves picked and chopped

25g pine nuts, lightly toasted, chopped

a splash of red wine vinegar

sea salt and black pepper

Finely chop the pork and place in a bowl. Ensure there is some fat with the pork to help the mix bind. Add the rest of the ingredients, mix and season with salt and pepper. Proceed as on page 30.

Ricotta, Peas & Mint

120g sheep or buffalo ricotta

50g frozen peas, defrosted

10 fresh mint leaves, roughly shredded

extra virgin olive oil

zest of ¼ lemon

sea salt and black pepper

Mix all the ingredients together and check the seasoning. Proceed as on page 30.

DUCK LIVER & PEDRO XIMÉNEZ PATÉ

This is our take on the classic chicken liver parfait. Duck livers have a richer flavour and more texture than chicken livers and are visually more appealing, as they're pinker, when turned into paté. Pedro Ximénez is a rich Spanish sherry which can now be found in most supermarkets. Its sticky sweetness works really well in this recipe. If duck livers are unavailable, use chicken livers instead. This is lovely served with a glass of off-dry sherry such as a Palo Cortado.

Serves 4

300g duck livers, trimmed, sinew removed

1 small shallot, diced

50ml Pedro Ximénez

1 teaspoon thyme leaves

170ml double cream

olive oil for cooking

sea salt and black pepper

Heat a non-stick pan over a high heat and add a lug of olive oil. Season the livers and sauté, along with the shallots, until the livers are nicely caramelised on both sides but still medium pink in the centre. This will take around 3 minutes. Immediately transfer the livers to a bowl to stop the cooking process.

Deglaze the sauté pan by adding the Pedro Ximénez and the thyme leaves. Bring to a boil, stirring and scraping the residue until it dissolves into the Pedro Ximénez. When reduced down a bit, add the cream and reduce by half. Turn off the heat and transfer the livers and the boozy cream to a food processor.

Blend for 4–5 minutes or until the paté is nice and smooth. Check the seasoning and then transfer the paté into 4 small serving pots. Ramekins are ideal. Cool down completely in the fridge. Take out of the fridge 10 minutes before serving. Serve with ciabatta crostini and some pickled guindillas or caperberries.

PORK RILLIONS

These devillishly moreish salty snacks originate from the southwest of France, but made the journey over the border into Spain a long time ago and can now be found in tapas bars the length and breadth of the land. As with most delicious things in life, they should be eaten in moderation. They are, after all, fried pieces of pork belly sprinkled liberally with sea salt! A glass of fresh-tasting, dry sherry is just the ticket to wash them down.

Serves 6

1kg pork belly, skin on, cut into small lardon-sized chunks

100g lard or duck fat

3 bay leaves

1 sprig thyme

3 cloves garlic, skin on, crushed

a little olive oil

sea salt

Heat a large ovenproof pan over a medium heat and add the lard or fat. When the fat is hot, add the pork belly. Season with sea salt and then cook for 5–7 minutes to colour the meat evenly and crisp up the skin. Throw in the bay, thyme and garlic and pour in a glass (about 200ml) of water. Bring the water to the boil and then lower to a simmer. Cook the pork belly slowly, turning from time to time, until the meat is nice and tender and the water has reduced. This should take about an hour but do add more water as needed: the pork is only done when completely tender.

In the meantime, preheat the oven to 180°C.

When tender, transfer the pork from the pan to a baking tray and drizzle with olive oil. Place in the oven and roast quickly for 10 minutes or so to crisp up the fat. Sprinkle liberally with sea salt and serve immediately.

CRISPY IBÉRICO PIGS' EARS

These piggy treats were born out of our bar snack development at Opera Tavern. Wanting a new take on the pub classic of pork scratchings, we experimented with the ears of the Ibérico pigs we use for other cuts and recipes. They have now become a firm favourite at Opera Tavern with customers and staff alike. Crispy, porky and salty – what's not to like? Regular pigs' ears are also perfectly adequate for this recipe and a good butcher will be happy to supply them to you, given a bit of notice.

Serves 6

6 medium pigs' ears, washed in cold running water for 10 minutes, then dried

2 cloves garlic, skin on, crushed

1 stem rosemary, leaves picked off, chopped

120g coarse salt

1.5 litres duck fat or pork lard, melted

60g plain flour

2 litres (approx.) vegetable oil for deep frying

Place the ears in a container along with the garlic and rosemary leaves and then sprinkle with salt, ensuring the ears are coated, top and bottom. Place the container in the fridge and leave the ears to cure for 4–5 hours. When they are ready, wash the ears in cold water and pat dry.

Pour the fat into a medium-sized saucepan and place over a low heat. Lower the ears into the fat, making sure they are completely submerged. Place a piece of baking paper on top. Cook the ears very slowly over a very low heat for about 3 hours or until the ears are soft and tender. Don't rush this process: if you cook the ears too quickly, they will burn. When the ears are ready, remove from the fat and drain well on kitchen paper. The fat can be used again for our pork belly recipe or more pigs' ears. With a sharp knife, slice the ears very finely into thin strips.

Heat the vegetable oil to 180°C in a deep fat fryer, or until a piece of bread fizzles and turns brown when dropped into a deep-sided pan. Toss the ear strips in the flour to give them a light coating and then shake off any excess. Fry the ears until golden brown and crispy. Drain the ears well on kitchen paper, transfer to a dish, and sprinkle liberally with sea salt. Leave to cool for 10 minutes before serving in little bowls.

Pinchos Morunos

Hailing from Andalucia, these grilled kebabs are traditionally made of pork or lamb marinated in paprika, garlic and oil and finished with a vigorous squeeze of lemon juice. At Opera Tavern, we've experimented with different meat-and-marinade combinations. We've given three versions here and it's lovely to serve all three at the same time. Serve the pinchos straight from the charcoal grill or barbecue, when they're lightly charred and deliciously sticky from the intense heat.

Duck Pinchos With Figs & Orange

Makes 8 skewers

8 x 12cm skewers, soaked in water

350g duck breast, skin on, diced into 3cm cubes

4 fresh figs, cut into 6 slices each

500ml orange juice

100ml Moscatel vinegar or white balsamic vinegar

½ lemon for squeezing

olive oil for cooking

sea salt and black pepper

A classic pairing of duck with orange and figs. The sweet fruit works well with the rich meat.

Alternate cubes of duck and slices of fig on the skewers, aiming for 3 pieces of each on each skewer. Place on a shallow tray.

Pour the orange juice and vinegar into a small saucepan and reduce over a high heat by two thirds or until slightly thickened. Allow the juice to cool, then pour over the pinchos. Leave to marinate in the fridge for a couple of hours.

Preheat the barbecue or grill to maximum.

Drain the excess marinade from the pinchos. Season and drizzle with olive oil. Place the pinchos under the grill or on the barbecue and cook for 2–3 minutes on each side or until the meat is nicely charred and medium. The meat should have a little spring in it when pressed with a finger. Allow the pinchos to rest in a warm spot. Then serve with some of the marinade spooned over and a squeeze of lemon.

Lamb & Kidney Pinchos With Smoked Paprika

Makes 8 skewers

8 x 12cm wooden skewers, soaked in water

350g leg of lamb, trimmed of fat, diced into 3cm cubes

4 lambs' kidneys, cut in half through the middle, white core removed

3 cloves garlic, finely chopped

4 teaspoons sweet smoked paprika

6 sprigs fresh thyme, leaves finely chopped

1 teaspoon ground cumin

100ml Cabernet Sauvignon vinegar or other red wine vinegar

300ml extra virgin olive oil

½ lemon for squeezing

sea salt and black pepper

IBÉRICO PORK PINCHOS WITH SMOKED PAPRIKA & CUMIN

Makes 8 skewers

8 x 12cm wooden skewers, soaked in cold water

500g Ibérico pork loin or good-quality rare breed pork loin, trimmed of most fat

4 teaspoons sweet smoked paprika

2 teaspoons cumin seeds, toasted

4 cloves garlic, finely chopped

100ml Cabernet Sauvignon vinegar or other red wine vinegar

300ml extra virgin olive oil

½ lemon for squeezing

sea salt and black pepper

Lambs' kidneys have great depth of flavour as well as providing a lovely textural contrast with the lamb leg. If you prefer not to use kidney, however, just double the quantity of diced lamb leg.

Cut each half kidney into 3 pieces. Alternate cubes of lamb leg and pieces of kidney on the skewers so that each skewer ends up with 4 pieces of lamb leg and 3 pieces of kidney. Lay the pinchos in a shallow tray.

In a mixing bowl, whisk together the garlic, paprika, thyme, cumin, vinegar and olive oil and then pour evenly over the skewers ensuring they are all well-covered. Place the tray in the fridge and marinate for a couple of hours. Turn the pinchos once during this time.

Follow the instructions as for the duck pinchos.

The classic version. If you are using Ibérico pork, the pinchos can be served rare. If using another breed of pork, cook until medium.

Dice the pork into approximately 3cm cubes and thread onto the skewers. There should be about 4 pieces on each skewer. Place the skewers in a shallow tray.

In a mixing bowl, whisk all the marinade ingredients – paprika, toasted cumin seeds, garlic, vinegar and olive oil – very well. Pour evenly over the pork. Turn the skewers to ensure they are all coated with the marinade and transfer to the fridge. Marinate for about 2 hours, turning the pork once during this time. Remove the pork from the fridge and scrape off the excess marinade.

Follow the instructions as for the duck pinchos.

THE INSIDE SCOOP

Max Halley is a part-time waiter at Opera Tavern. He is also a writer, broadcaster and designer.

I give people a good time for a living. I loosen them up and give them what they want. I make people's day. I keep my clothes on and I'm not Heidi Fleiss. Guess what I do. I'm a waiter.

Waitering is often undervalued and underpaid. Regarded as a job for resting actors and transient nobodies, there are many disillusioned people in the trade. Our staff however, myself included, are happy to come to work at the Salt Yard restaurants. Big smiles are kept firmly in place by generous pay, proper training and free wine after work. It's not rocket science and it's not hippy claptrap: happy staff make happy customers. Most of the time.

The light on the lift turns green and I whir into action. It's Friday night and it's busy. I give table 52 their first round of tapas and walk across the room, glancing back to make sure they're happy with the food. We are not only what and where we eat, but how we eat. If someone picks up their cutlery straight away, they're pleased with the food and all is good. If the cutlery stays down, something's amiss.

I drift around the room looking relaxed, but like a swan, I'm working flat out underneath. I stop to talk to the couple on table 54 and offer them an aperitif. 'Oh God,' the woman says. 'I can't see the wood for the trees.' I recommend a Campari Spritz because it's what I would have. Slightly bitter but fizzy and light; it kicks things off perfectly. People suspect the aperitif. They unfairly think it's a ruse to rack up the bill —

but it's anything but. It preps the palate for the coming onslaught and prevents the wine being ordered before the food. Have a glass, by all means, but please don't commit to a bottle. You could end up eating your delicate ceviche and drinking a huge tannic red.

The manager seats a table of slightly rowdy men and they immediately wave me over. 'Pick us the good stuff,' one of them says. 'Don't worry how much it costs.' Talk turns to wine and I suggest going by the glass. With a choice of ten sherries, nine reds, nine whites, two rosés, fizz and pudding wines, there is a perfect match for every dish. Not that bothered, they order a bottle. I nip off, come back, pour a little for the man who ordered and ask him to make sure he likes it. 'And what are you going to do if I don't?' he replies. I tell him 'I'm going to take it away and get something else.' It's not enough that it isn't corked. If you're paying for it, it's only fair that you like it.

I turn and hear someone coming up the stairs. A nervous young man arrives and quietly tells me he has a table booked. I check the reservation sheet, take him to his table and fetch a glass of water before he passes out. He leans forward, rubs his temples and runs a finger round his collar. He tilts his head and taps his foot. Yes ladies and gentlemen, it's a first date! The date arrives and the introduction's awkward. My boy's in trouble, he's floundering. I steamroller in and suggest a glass of fizz. 'Oh yes,' she says, 'what a wonderful idea.' Glasses clink and they're off. A little later he's ready to order wine and clutches the list so close to his chest that I have to lean down to see where he's pointing. It's the house red, our cheapest bottle. 'The Grenache,' I say, looking to the girl. 'Fantastic.' I take two steps and turn back. 'It can be a little tight at first. Would you like me to decant it for you?' Decant it? He's over the moon. 'Oh, definitely,' he says, confidence rising, looking like he's won the lottery. 'I mean, if you think it needs to open up a bit...' Off stage, I unscrew the lid and fill the decanter, returning to pour them a glass. He surveys the scene like Butch Cassidy. They are the only table in the restaurant with a decanter and people are impressed.

As the night rolls on, bills are settled, the restaurant empties and we clean up and close. I head off to a restaurant in Chinatown that I've frequented since student days. When I walk in, the staff resist the temptation to shout at me, as they do all the other customers. A trio of girls stagger in a little worse for wear. 'How many? Three? Upstairs!' the man on the door yells. 'But we were hoping – '. 'Yeah, yeah,' he says waving his hand dismissively, 'downstairs closed. UPSTAIRS!'

The waiter comes over and slams a pot of jasmine tea on the table in front of me. 'What do you want?' he barks. Before I can answer, he sighs, 'The usual, I suppose,' and stalks away throwing disapproving looks at my fellow diners. I sit on my own, eating the same dish, at the same table, three times a week. Poacher turned gamekeeper. The food isn't great and the atmosphere's terrible but after a long day smiling at everyone, the waiters here are just what I need. Their apathy is a constant reminder of why I choose to work at the Opera Tavern, where we don't ruin days, we make them.

CURED & PICKLED

Go into any bar in Spain or Italy and you'll probably find a menu chalked up on a blackboard listing various types of cured meat and fish to accompany your drink. There may well be a leg of ham on the bar, which the waiter is in the process of carving into delicious, wafer-thin slices.

Charcuterie and curing are taken very seriously indeed in both countries, and producers are revered for their skill and consistency. We've visited the almost cathedral-like curing houses of Salamanca in Spain, and those of Parma, Italy, where thousands of legs of ham are piled under salt, washed, dried, and then matured in cellars, and rows upon rows of salchichon or salami are hung to develop their flavours. It's fascinating to observe the centuries-old practice of curing in action and see how the meats are monitored by the curers with a devotion that borders on the religious.

Curing also extends to fish and even vegetables – the drying, salting and smoking processes involved were originally developed to save or preserve food in the days before we had decent refrigeration. In Britain, we've long cured our own bacon, hams and kippers but don't have a strong tradition of charcuterie, like on the Continent. However, there are now a few UK artisan producers, such as Trealy Farm in Wales, who are applying Spanish and Italian methods of curing to our high quality British meat. The results are excellent and we've worked with them to

make a bespoke Salt Yard chilli and marjoram salami. On any given day at our restaurants you'll find beautifully produced, unusual artisan charcuterie from Spain and Italy, as well as our own meat and fish products that we've cured in-house. Delicate salamis from Alto Adige; fragrant fennel pollen salami from Umbria; spicy chorizos from León or our own five-year cured Jamón Ibérico de Bellota from Salamanca might be on the menu. There may be home-cured duck breast flavoured with fennel, a refreshing house salt cod salad with blood orange, home-cured Calabrian style 'nduja or mackerel escabeche.

Following simple instructions and techniques, it's possible to produce stunning results in your own home too – anything from salt cod to your own salami. Home curing is hugely satisfying, but one thing you do need is time as some meat and fish take several weeks to cure. If making chorizo, pancetta and salami, you'll need a good place to hang and dry the sausages; somewhere humid, dark and breezy, such as a cellar or shed with air movement, is ideal. At the restaurants we hang our meats in the cool, humid vaults under the pavements and direct a fan at them to keep the air circulating. All purpose curing salt, which makes the charcuterie safe to eat after weeks of curing, can be bought from butchers or online. The only other thing to consider, as with all recipes in this book, is to buy the best products you can afford. Don't scrimp on ingredients – it's the cardinal sin.

BEEF KHILI

This wonderful dried beef came to Spain from Morocco during the time of the Moors. Traditionally, beef strips were marinated and then left to dry under a baking hot sun. If you're not so lucky as to have the sun beating down outside, a warm, dry spot near the oven will do. Khili is a fantastic pre-dinner snack, evocative of exotic climes with its cumin, chilli and coriander flavouring. Alternatively, you can fry the khili till crisp in olive oil. It's great tossed in a chicory salad with a lemon and mustard dressing.

Makes about 240g khili

500g beef skirt or bavette, trimmed of sinew but with some fat left intact

1 Spanish onion, peeled, grated

4 cloves garlic, peeled, finely chopped

1 teaspoon dried chilli flakes

1 teaspoon ground cumin

1 teaspoon ground coriander

20g sea salt

4 grinds black pepper

a squeeze of lemon juice

a splash of cold water

Place the beef on a chopping board. With a long, sharp knife, carefully slice along the grain, cutting the meat into strips. Take your time, making sure the strips are long and thin. When sliced, check that all the strips are of the same thickness. If there are any lumps, bash them out with the flat side of a large knife.

Place the beef in a bowl and add all the remaining ingredients. Mix very well. Transfer the bowl to the fridge and leave for an hour, turning the beef 2 or 3 times.

Preheat the oven to 80°C.

Remove the khili from the fridge and wash the marinade off. Lay the strips on a cooling rack placed on top of a baking tray. Make sure the strips don't overlap or they won't dry evenly. Place the khili in the oven for about 30 minutes or until the meat has started to shrink and tighten. Remove and place in a warm spot, covered loosely with foil, for about 12 hours or until the beef has shrunk and is hard to the touch. The khili will have the consistency of beef jerky and be quite chewy. The flavours are quite intense!

BRESAOLA

Bresaola is the classic cured beef topside that's served all over Italy. We love to make this at the restaurants. The results are always spot on and you can really taste the difference between this and commercially produced versions. There's a clarity to the flavours. It retains its beefiness while being perfectly balanced by the acidity of the wine and the spiciness of the aromatics. Make several at a time, as they keep for months. It's a real treat to discover some bresaola in the fridge when you thought there was nothing else left.

Makes about 3kg of bresaola

3–4kg good-quality beef topside or silverside

For the brine:

800g coarse sea salt

10 sprigs thyme

8 fresh bay leaves

6 star anise

2 tablespoons black peppercorns

zest of 2 lemons

zest of 2 oranges

6 garlic cloves, crushed

2 teaspoons fennel seeds

3 fresh chillies, cut in half lengthwise

1 bottle good red wine

Trim the meat of any sinew or fat if necessary. Your butcher will do this for you, if asked. Mix together all the ingredients for the brine and pour into a plastic container that will also house the meat comfortably. Place the meat in the brine and leave in a cool place for 5 days. During the 5-day curing period, turn the meat daily to ensure an even brine.

After the fifth day, remove the beef, pat dry and wrap in a clean tea towel or muslin cloth. Tie each end securely with string. You now need to hang the beef in a cool, airy spot like a shed or even outside on a porch – just make sure it's sheltered from the rain. Leave the beef to hang for around 12–14 days until it's firm to the touch.

Remove the bresaola from the cloth and trim the ends. It's now ready to slice. If you have a bacon slicer this is perfect, as bresaola should be cut wafer-thin. Otherwise a sharp knife will do.

Bresaola is delicious served the classic way – with lemon, rocket and olive oil – but you could experiment with Parmesan, a little fresh goat's curd, or even some pomegranate seeds.

Tip: To store, rewrap the bresaola in cloth, never cling film, so the beef can breathe and not sweat. If, after curing, you see white mould on the surface of the bresaola, just rub it off with a cloth dipped in a little vinegar. It's perfectly harmless.

Chorizo

Chorizo, the much-loved staple of Spanish cuisine, owes its deep, red colour and unique flavour to the king of Spanish spices, smoked paprika. Here we use both sweet and hot smoked paprikas and throw in some crushed fennel seeds as well for a hint of aniseed. Once you've made this chorizo, we hope you'll never turn back to shop-bought sausages as the flavours here are so fresh and pure. As always, use the best-quality pork you can find. All good delis normally stock good-quality smoked paprikas.

Makes around 16–18 sausages

You will need a mincer with a sausage-stuffing attachment

400g pork belly, cut into small chunks

400g pork shoulder, cut into small chunks

4 teaspoons curing salt

3 tablespoons sweet smoked paprika

2 tablespoons hot smoked paprika

1½ tablespoons fennel seeds, crushed

30g hog casing, washed, soaked in cold water

Ensure the meat is thoroughly chilled before mincing. Feed the pork meat through the mincer, using a fine blade, into a mixing bowl and then mix in all the other ingredients. Knead the meat with your hands to incorporate everything together fully.

Fit the small sausage nozzle on the mincer and thread on the hog casing. Feed the chorizo mix into the feeder and slowly stuff the casing. It's good to have two people at this stage: one to feed in the meat and the other to hold the length of the sausage. Expel all excess air from the sausage by pricking the skin with a toothpick. When all the meat has filled the casing, tie a knot in one end of the sausage with butcher's twine and then link the sausages at regular intervals, about every 15cm. Linking involves pinching the sausage and twisting 3 times, alternating the direction in which you twist each time, until you end up with a chain of sausages. Tie a knot in the other end. Tie more butcher's twine round each link to secure in place.

Now hang the sausages in a humid, cool, dark area like a shed or garage. Hang the chorizo until it's started to firm but is still a little soft when squeezed. This will take about a month, but start checking it every few days towards the end of this time to monitor how it's firming up.

Slice your chorizo and serve as part of a charcuterie board, or use for its fantastic flavour, in any number of dishes, such as stews, soups, with meat, squid or lentils.

'NDUJA

This spicy, soft salami, or paté, originates from the sun-soaked region of Calabria in southern Italy. It's not for the faint-hearted as it packs a serious chilli kick, as you can probably guess from the chilli content in the recipe. Although it takes a good month to cure, it's quite soft and you can treat it as you would a paté, spreading it on hot, buttered toast or crostini. Serve this 'nduja with something sweet like sherry-macerated raisins or caramelised apples to help balance its fieriness.

Makes approximately
16 small salami

You will need a mincer with a sausage-stuffing attachment

200g pork shoulder, cut into small chunks

400g fatty pork belly, cut into small chunks

200g fresh red chillies, finely chopped

20g hot smoked paprika

22g all purpose curing salt

1 teaspoon black peppercorns, crushed

1 teaspoon fennel seeds, crushed

1 teaspoon fresh marjoram leaves, chopped

30g hog casing, washed, soaked in water

Ensure your meat is thoroughly chilled before mincing. Feed the pork meats through the mincer, using a fine blade, into a mixing bowl and then mix in all the other ingredients. Knead the meat with the palms of your hands to incorporate everything together fully.

Fit the small sausage nozzle on the mincer and thread on the hog casing. Feed the salami mix into the feeder and slowly stuff the casing. It's good to have two people at this stage: one to feed in the meat and the other to hold the length of the sausage. Expel all excess air from the sausage by pricking the skin with a toothpick. When all the meat has filled the casing, tie a knot in one end of the sausage with butcher's twine and then link the sausages at regular intervals, about every 15cm. Linking involves pinching the sausage and twisting 3 times, alternating the direction in which you twist each time, until you end up with a chain of sausages. Tie a knot in the other end. Tie more butcher's twine round each link to secure in place.

Now hang the sausages in a humid, cool, dark area like a shed or garage. Hang the 'nduja until it has started to firm but is still a little soft when squeezed. This will take about a month – take a look every few days to monitor how it is firming up.

IBÉRICO PIG'S HEAD TERRINE

This is not a recipe for the faint-hearted but it is very satisfying and something you might tackle over a long, rainy weekend! Firstly, you'll need to source a pig's head. Your butcher will be able to help you, given some notice. You'll also need time. The pig's head needs to be washed for a few hours, then brined, cooked, picked and finally, pressed until set. After that, you can eat it. A pot large enough to hold the pig's head during brining and cooking and a terrine mould with a lid for pressing are also required.

Makes 1 terrine or 12–16 servings

Brine for the terrine:

16 litres water

2.8kg rock salt

1.8kg demerara sugar

10 bay leaves

10 sprigs thyme

2 teaspoons juniper berries

2 teaspoons peppercorns

For the terrine:

1 Ibérico pig's head or regular breed

2 leeks, split, washed

4 carrots, peeled

6 sprigs thyme

5 bay leaves

2 sprigs rosemary

3 white onions, peeled

6 small shallots, peeled, finely chopped

½ bunch flat-leaf parsley, chopped

1 tablespoon capers

2 tablespoons Cabernet Sauvignon vinegar

To make the brine, place all the ingredients in a large pan and bring briefly to the boil, whisking until the salt and sugar have dissolved. Let cool. Place the pig's head under cold, running water for about 2 hours, or until the water runs clear, to wash off any impurities and traces of blood. Put the head in the brine, placing a weighted plate on top to keep it submerged. Leave the brine in the fridge or a cool spot for 24 hours. After this time, wash the head for 30 minutes under cold, running water to desalinate.

Place the pig's head back in the washed pot, cover with cold water and add the leeks, carrots, thyme, bay, rosemary and onions. Bring to the boil and then reduce to a simmer. Cook the head slowly for 3–4 hours, skimming off any impurities that rise to the surface. The head is ready when the meat has just started to fall from the bone and the jaw has dislocated.

Whilst the head is cooking, moisten the inside of the terrine mould and line with 3 layers of cling film, leaving enough overhang so that you can fold the flaps over to seal the meat once it's in. Press the cling film into the sides of the mould ensuring it fits snugly and that there are no air bubbles.

When the head is cooked, carefully transfer to a plate and cool for 20 minutes. Strain 2 litres of the cooking liquor into a small saucepan, reduce over a low heat to 400ml stock and reserve. Now remove the skin and meat from the pig's skull, which will come away fairly easily. When you pick the meat from the skull, try not to shred it too

much, aiming instead for small, whole pieces. You need about 5 times as much pink meat as fat and skin for the terrine. Discard the superfluous fat and skin. Place the picked meat and fat in a bowl and add the capers, parsley, shallots, vinegar and the reduced cooking liquor. Mix well and taste for seasoning. Press the meat carefully into the terrine ensuring it fills the mould fully and that there are no gaps. Slightly overfill the mould as it's about to be pressed. Fold over the cling film flaps. Pierce the cling film several times on top with a knife to allow excess juices to escape during pressing. Put the terrine on a tray and cover with the lid with 2 or 3 tins on top to ensure a good press. Put in the fridge for at least 6 hours or overnight.

When ready, the terrine will be completely chilled and firm to the touch. Leave at room temperature for 20 minutes and then turn the terrine out onto a chopping board with the cling film still intact. Slice off what you need with a long, sharp knife. Serve with toasted sourdough and guindilla peppers. The remaining terrine will keep in the fridge for 5 days.

SPICED SALAMI

A simple cured sausage for beginners. It's resistant to less than ideal curing conditions, so it's hard to go wrong when making it. Use good-quality pork with a high fat content like Old Spot. You could try varying the spices, replacing the chilli with ground fennel or coriander seeds or a combination of the two. There's nothing like seeing the fruits of your labour when sausage-making and home-curing for the first time, so give it a go!

Makes around 16–18 sausages

You will need a mincer with a sausage-stuffing attachment

400g pork shoulder, off the bone, cut into chunks

400g pork belly, skin removed, cut into chunks

150ml red wine

5 cloves garlic, finely chopped

1 teaspoon ground cinnamon

1 teaspoon chilli flakes

23g all purpose curing salt

½ teaspoon ground black pepper

30g hog casing, soaked, rinsed in cold water

Ensure the meat is very cold before mincing. Set up your mincer and fit an attachment with small holes. Carefully pass the meats through the mincer into a metal bowl. Add the wine, garlic, cinnamon, chilli, salt and pepper. Mix very well and knead briefly to incorporate fully, working the meat and flavourings together.

Attach the small sausage nozzle to the mincer and thread on the hog casing. Feed the salami mix into the feeder and slowly stuff the casing. It's good to have two people at this stage: one to feed in the meat and the other to hold the length of the sausage. Expel all excess air from the sausage by pricking the skin with a toothpick. When all the meat has filled the casing, tie a knot in one end of the sausage with butcher's twine and then link the sausages at regular intervals, about every 15cm. Linking involves pinching the sausage and twisting 3 times, alternating the direction in which you twist each time, until you end up with a chain of sausages. Tie a knot in the other end. Tie more butcher's twine round each link to secure in place.

You now need to hang the sausages in a humid, cool, dark area like a shed or garage. Hang the cacciatore until nice and firm with a touch of mould. This will take about 1 month to 6 weeks.

When ready, serve on your charcuterie board or very thinly sliced with some cheese and mustard fruits for an amazing sandwich.

PANCETTA

You'll get a great deal of satisfaction from making your own pancetta. It's incredibly simple to prepare and, as with most charcuterie, all it takes is some time, patience and space to hang it in. Pancetta is used widely in Italian cooking and its pronounced salty flavour forms the backbone of many Italian recipes. When choosing your pork belly, consider its fattiness as that's where most of the flavour is: the fattier, the better. Old Spot has a good layering of fat and produces the finest pork belly meat.

Makes about 1.5kg of pancetta

2kg fresh pork belly with a good fat-to-meat ratio, skin and ribs removed

4 sprigs rosemary, picked, leaves reserved

110g all purpose curing salt

3 cloves garlic, peeled, finely chopped

2 tablespoons muscovado sugar

3 tablespoons freshly ground black pepper

1 nutmeg, finely grated

1 tablespoon juniper berries, crushed

1 tablespoon fennel seeds, crushed

Combine all the ingredients except the pork in a bowl and mix well. Place the pork in a large fridge-proof container and pour in the salt mix. Rub the salt mix evenly all over the pork, not forgetting underneath. Cover the container and place the pork in the fridge for about a week. During this time, turn the pork over every other day and redistribute the salt mix.

At the end of the week, check the pork. If it feels firm to the touch, then it's ready to hang up and dry. If it feels soft, then leave for a couple more days in the fridge. When cured, rinse the pancetta under cold, running water for a few minutes to wash off the excess salt and then dry well on kitchen paper.

Lay out a clean tea towel and place the pancetta on top. Wrap the pork tightly and tie both ends of the cloth with twine, making sure the pork is secure and completely covered.

Now hang your pork in a dark, humid spot with good air circulation, such as a shed or garage. Make sure it's not touching anything. After 6 days, check the pork to see if it's firm but yielding. If it is, take off the cloth, wrap in cling film and transfer to the fridge until ready to use. The pancetta will be fine in the fridge for up to 3 weeks.

DUCK WITH FENNEL, CINNAMON & ORANGE

Fennel, orange and cinnamon are often used when cooking duck, so why not when curing? This recipe was developed with this thinking in mind and it works a treat. Fat is very important in the preparation of charcuterie and when salted is exquisite. Ducks are naturally fatty birds so are wonderful when cured. The fattier the duck breast you use here, the better. When hanging the ducks, you'll need an airy space like a shed or garage that's sheltered from the rain. A hook in the roof will also come in useful.

Makes about 300g

2 fatty duck breasts

2 tablespoons fennel seeds

200g coarse salt

120g granulated sugar

zest of 1 orange and the rest of the orange sliced thinly

1 tablespoon ground cinnamon

olive oil

Trim the duck breasts of any sinew. Score the skin with a very sharp knife but ensure you do not cut into the flesh.

Mix together the salt cure: fennel, salt, sugar, zest and cinnamon. Place the duck breasts skin-side up in a plastic container and pour over the cure mix. Massage into the duck, ensuring the breasts are covered. Layer the orange slices on top of the duck. Cover the container with a lid or cling film and transfer to the fridge for 12 hours. Turn the breasts once during the marinating process.

After marinating, remove the breasts from the cure and wash under cold, running water for 20 minutes. Pat the breasts dry with kitchen paper. You will now need 2 new J-cloths and some twine. Place a breast on each cloth and wrap. Secure each end with the twine and then tie a piece of twine at 2 intervals around the breast to secure.

Hang the breasts in a cool, dry spot for approximately 5–6 days. When ready, the breast will feel firm when squeezed between finger and thumb but slightly softer in the centre.

Remove the breast from the cloth and rub lightly with olive oil. Wrap in cling film and chill until ready to slice. Serve as part of a charcuterie board, or in a salad.

BEETROOT-CURED SALMON

WITH CUMIN & CORIANDER

Cured salmon is associated with Scandinavian gravadlax. We've adapted the traditional recipe by adding grated beetroot for colour and freshly ground coriander and cumin seeds for exotic spicing. Finally, we add a little orange juice and zest for extra zing. The citrus and aromatics used here produce a sweet, balanced cure. Visually, the salmon has a slightly psychedelic appearance with its bright red and orange layers. Make a whole side as it takes 24 hours to make and will keep in the fridge for about 10 days.

Serves 12–16

1 side of salmon, (approx. 1kg), pin bones removed, skin scaled

140g caster sugar

100g sea salt

2 medium beetroots, peeled, coarsely grated

1 tablespoon coriander seeds, freshly ground in a mortar and pestle

1 tablespoon cumin seeds, freshly ground in a mortar and pestle

zest and juice of 2 small oranges

Firstly cut the salmon fillet in 2 widthways and with a very sharp knife, score the skin of the thicker parts of the fish. Place all the other ingredients in a mixing bowl and combine together very well to make a wet salt mix.

Find a dish large and deep enough for the 2 salmon fillets to sit side by side. Place half the salt mix in the dish, spread out evenly, and then lay the fillets on top of the salt, skin-side down. Firmly press the salmon down into the salt and then top with the remaining salt mix. Ensure each fillet is evenly-coated and packed firmly with the salt. Place a heavy plate on top of the fillets to weigh them down and then wrap the whole dish very tightly in cling film. Transfer to the fridge for 24 hours. About half way through the curing process, unwrap the salmon, remove the plate and turn the fish, pressing the other side firmly into the salt. Reposition the plate, wrap tightly again and put back in the fridge for the remaining time.

After the 24 hours are up, remove the salmon from the fridge and wash off the excess salt for a few minutes under cold, running water. Pat dry on kitchen paper. With a sharp knife, thinly slice the salmon from the flesh to the skin. Tuck the knife under each slice to release from the skin, which is inedible. We suggest serving the salmon at room temperature with some lemon and buttered bread.

MACKEREL ESCABECHE

Making escabeche is the Spanish way to pickle. In Britain we would souse. It's really important to use top-quality vinegar and olive oil for escabeche as these will be the predominant flavours of this beautiful dish. Of course, whatever you are pickling should also be supremely fresh. At the restaurants, we pickle meats and game in season as they stand up well to the full flavours of the marinade. Bear this in mind when pickling fish too: strong-flavoured fish such as mackerel, mullet and sea trout work best.

Serves 4–6 as a tapa

3 fillets mackerel, (approx. 200g each), pin bones removed, cut in half widthwise

1 carrot, peeled, finely sliced

1 banana shallot, peeled, finely sliced

2 bay leaves

1 teaspoon coriander seeds

150ml extra virgin olive oil, such as Arbequina

250ml Moscatel vinegar or white balsamic vinegar

6 saffron strands

a squeeze of lemon

olive oil for frying

sea salt and black pepper

Place the carrots, shallots, bay and coriander seeds in a saucepan and pour over the extra virgin olive oil and vinegar. Bring slowly to the boil, add the saffron and season to taste. Turn down the heat and simmer for 2 minutes. Turn off the heat and leave to stand.

Heat a non-stick pan over a high heat and add a lug of olive oil. Season the mackerel pieces and place in the pan, skin-side down. When the skin has browned and crisped, remove the fish from the pan and transfer to a container. Pour over the marinade and add a squeeze of lemon juice. Ensure the fillets are completely submerged. Cover the container and transfer to the fridge for at least 2 hours, and up to 3 weeks.

Serve the mackerel escabeche at room temperature with some of the marinade drizzled on top, some crostini and a green salad.

SALT COD

No European cookbook would be complete without the inclusion of salt cod, or bacalao – and there are few things better than your own cured cod. Curing times vary depending on how you want to eat the salt cod. A lightly cured, semi-raw bacalao is superb thinly sliced over a fennel and orange salad and drizzled with good Ligurian olive oil. Cod cured a little longer can be cooked lightly in milk and mixed into mashed potatoes to make a brandade or into béchamel to make croquetas (see page 64). Seriously delicious.

Produces about 450g salt cod

800g fresh cod or pollack (filleted weight), skin intact, lightly washed, patted dry

250g rock salt

4 cloves garlic, peeled, crushed, chopped

5 sprigs fresh thyme, roughly chopped

You'll need a plastic container big enough to hold the cod and the salt. Sprinkle half of the salt into the container and lay the cod on top, skin-side down. Cover with the remaining salt, garlic and thyme. Ensure the salt mix fully covers the cod on all sides so there is an even cure. Place a lid on the container and pop in the fridge.

The cod can now be left in the fridge for anything between 1 hour and 12 days, depending on the recipe you wish to follow. We give guidelines below but you'll have to exercise your own judgment to some extent, as each piece of fish will take a shorter or longer time to cure depending on how thick it is. Turn the fish once every 24 hours.

If you want to simply firm up and very lightly cure the fish, leave in salt for about an hour and then wash off the excess in cold, running water for 10 minutes. Slice and serve in a salad or pan-roast.

To make fritters, brandade or croquetas, curing for 24 hours is ideal. The fish will be nicely seasoned with a strong, salty perfume which is not overbearing. After 24 hours in salt, you should wash the fish in cold, running water for about an hour or so.

If you want to heavily cure the cod, then leave it in salt for 10–12 days. During this process, turn the cod once. After curing, rinse the cod under cold, running water for about 4–5 hours to fully desalinate. You could now poach the cod in milk or water for a few minutes and then grate over pasta or risotto.

THE GRAPE MIGRATION

By Simon Mullins

The sign on the dirt track leading to the winery's front door was wooden, rickety and weather-beaten. It read: 'Beware of the Rattlesnakes'. I'd just travelled 5,500 miles from London to the Santa Cruz Mountains, California. The last 20 miles of my journey had taken me up a winding, unkempt road, packed with hairpin bends. Narrowly avoiding collision at each turn, my car had climbed high over the valley below. The last stretch of the journey felt the longest and most dangerous – and then, when I thought I was safe, there was the rattlesnake sign waiting to greet me.

The winery I was visiting, Ridge Vineyards, sat on top of a ridge that overlooked the Pacific to the west and the Sierra Nevada to the east. The views were breath-taking. This wonderful place had been named Monte Bello by the Italian immigrant families who came here in the mid-19th century. Their voyage had been far longer and more treacherous than mine. Today, only two things remain as a reminder of their presence: a small crumbling ruin of a chapel and row upon row of glorious vines. As I soaked up my surroundings, I pondered what those early settlers had been through to get to this spot. One thing I knew for sure: they had brought vines with them all the way from Italy. Making, drinking and enjoying wine is at the heart of European culture, and so the immigrants had carefully transported their vines thousands of miles to be a part of their life in the new world.

This got me thinking: wine is amazing. Not just because of its wonderful variety, its pleasing effects and the ease of social interaction it facilitates. But also because of its long history and its incredible journey westwards – which have gone hand in hand with the spread of civilisation. The history of wine is woven into the history of humanity. It's been a jaunt of many millennia that man and vine have shared together.

Over 10,000 years ago, when most of us were roaming the earth nomad-style, one or two enlightened souls struck upon how to make wine. It's almost impossible to pinpoint exactly when and where grapes were first trodden to produce alcohol, but it's thought that the first wines came from somewhere between the Black and the Caspian Seas. It's there that the wild vine is indigenous. It can be found growing in crevices on rocky outcrops, hanging over steep-sided river gorges – in short, in all the hardiest of places.

The wild vine was first cultivated during the shift from nomadic to settled lifestyles, as communities began to prosper and trade to flourish. Trade included wine, and the enjoyment of the golden or ruby-coloured liquid became central to ceremony and celebration. The arrival of a newborn, the feast when trade was good, the welcoming of friendly folk from another region – all of these occasions called for many an amphora. Culture and humanity were evolving and wine was being washed down to celebrate.

Wine's place at the core of civilisation can be glimpsed in various art forms over the centuries. The 5000-year-old Sumerian artefact known as the Standard of Ur depicts images of War and Peace in mosaic – and Peace is represented by the drinking of wine at a banquet. One of the oldest known literary documents, the Epic of Gilgamesh, relates how wine from the enchanted

garden brought the drinker the gift of immortality. Homer tells how Odysseus outwitted the Cyclops by getting him passed-out drunk. Meanwhile, the shield Achilles carried into battle at Troy bore scenes of a grape harvest. I could go on...

Wine has also long been considered sacred. The ancient Egyptians thought jars of wine, placed in the tombs of their dead, carefully vintage-dated and initialled by the winemaker, were essential for ensuring a merry journey into the afterlife. And the ancient Greeks, of course, had Dionysus, the god of wine, who worshipped the drink high up on Olympus.

Coming back down to earth, when the ancient Greeks invaded Sicily and Southern Italy in the eighth century BC, they named the area Oenotria, or land of vines. They brought more efficient, intensive agricultural methods to Italy and most likely the first stake-trained vineyards too. Wine production soon spread across the rest of Italy, Spain and France. The Greeks were succeeded by the Romans, empires came and went, and as ideas and cultures morphed and moved west, so too did the vine. At each stop and with each new vineyard planted, the grapes mutated to suit their new location, as did the character of the wine. The march of the vine headed north through France up into Champagne, where in the 17th century a Benedictine monk named Dom Pérignon famously invented the first sparkling wine. Vines crossed the Alps into Switzerland, Austria and Germany and more recently have travelled across oceans to the Americas, South Africa, Australia and New Zealand. Mutations of grapes that originated many thousands of years ago in countries like Georgia and Iraq are now being cultivated as far away California and Chile. What a journey it has been to get the vine to the ridge overlooking the Pacific!

As for me, I'd come to California to see how indigenous Italian and Spanish grape varieties tasted when made here. The trip there was another part of my journey of discovery and that's what enjoying wine is all about: exploration and discovery. Our wine lists at the restaurants offer a constantly changing tour of the delicious wines that are being made in Spain and Italy. We've limited our selection to these two countries – though 'limited' may be the wrong word for such a kaleidoscope of choice! Today, Italy abounds with thousands of grape varieties, of which only 800 are officially documented, while Spain is rediscovering ancient, almost extinct varieties. One can now find a multitude of new and old producers from both countries making wines of real character that reflect their culture and place of origin. So I urge you to embark on your own journey of discovery. Explore, experiment, and most importantly, have fun. Just beware of those rattlesnakes.

FISH

Nothing excites our chefs more than the beautiful specimens of fish and shellfish we receive in our kitchens every morning, direct from Cornwall and beyond. Our suppliers are pedantic about choosing the freshest seafood available and deliver overnight to ensure it reaches us at its best. We make the most of our bounty and an eclectic mix of fish and shellfish features on our menus. There's usually octopus, perhaps chargrilled or a la Gallega, and often deep-fried or sautéed baby squid. Fresh crab spiked with chilli and marjoram and steamed wild sea bream, both caught off the Cornish coast, are popular, as are butter-roasted hake, steamed clams with parsley and salt cod croquetas. We give our own twist to Venetian cicchetti by serving super fresh slices of fish cured with little more than a squeeze of lemon juice and a sprinkling of Maldon sea salt.

Spain and Italy hold seafood in high esteem and you only have to go to a local market to see the most amazing displays of

fish, crustaceans, squid and octopus artfully arranged on packed ice. The dazzling colours make fish counters on the Continent a sight to behold, unlike those you find in your average British supermarket. As a nation, our interest in fish has really only developed recently, as, despite the ubiquitous fish and chips, we've generally always favoured meat. This is a great shame as British coastal waters boast some of the world's finest seafood, and yet, we export over 85% of our yearly haul to Spain! Recent upsurges in fish sales suggest we're starting to acquire more of a taste for the sea, but we've got some way to go before it's as common to pop out to buy a piece of fish for dinner as pick up a packet of sausages.

At the restaurants, we try to source as much of our fish from British coastal waters as possible, but inevitably, due to the Spanish and Italian nature of our tapas, we also source from seas further away, such as the Mediterranean. Our trusty UK suppliers, Matthew Stevens & Son and Coast Seafood, based in Cornwall and Dorset respectively, have the same ethos as we do. It's all about using the best quality fish caught in the most humane and sustainable manner, with a leaning towards lesser known varieties and a passion for seasonality. Some of our newer suppliers are starting to import some weird and wonderful specimens from Spain just for us: fresh white and black anchovies, beautifully sweet red gambas and the prehistoric-looking percebes, or goose barnacles, that require a sharp press and twist to release their delicious pink flesh.

When buying seafood, freshness is paramount. A good rule of thumb is if the fish looks fresh and healthy and doesn't smell fishy, but clean and briney, then it's fresh. The eyes of the fish should be bright, not sunken and dull. Build a good relationship with your fishmonger, so that he or she can alert you to the freshest fish and advise you on sustainability and cooking times.

MUSSELS

WITH CHERRY TOMATOES, BORLOTTI BEANS & BASIL

Borlotti beans are a favourite at our restaurants when in season between February and June. We love their multicoloured jackets, buttery texture and sweet, nutty flavour. The beans have a natural affiliation with tomatoes and fresh herbs but adding them to a shellfish dish is quite unusual. It certainly works though: the borlotti bean sauce gives this steamed mussel dish substance and heartiness. All you need is a hunk of bread on the side to mop up the juices.

Serves 4 as a starter or light main or 6–8 as a tapa

500g mussels, bearded, washed

1 banana shallot, chopped

2 cloves garlic, peeled, finely chopped

2 small red chillies, deseeded, chopped

300ml fish stock (see Basics)

200g cherry tomatoes, quartered

100ml dry white wine

350g cooked borlotti beans

30g unsalted butter

a small handful of basil leaves

olive oil for cooking

lemon juice to taste

sea salt and black pepper

Heat a medium-sized saucepan over a medium heat. Add a lug of olive oil followed by the chopped shallots and garlic. Sweat them down and then add the chilli and the mussels. Pour in the wine and steam the mussels until they open. Remove the mussels from the pan and reserve. Discard any that have not opened.

Reduce the wine until it's syrupy and then add the fish stock, tomatoes and borlotti beans. Reduce by half, until the sauce has thickened and the tomatoes have broken down into the sauce. Stir in the butter and half the basil and season with salt, pepper and lemon juice.

Toss the mussels in the sauce to warm through and then divide between serving bowls. Scatter over the remaining basil leaves and serve.

Try a Vermentino from Sardinia for a fresh match.

SALT COD FRITTERS

WITH ORANGE ALIOLI

Evocative of summer dining in Seville, these fritters are perfect for tapas or a canapé party. Piping hot from the fryer and dipped in a punchy, citrusy alioli, they are quite irresistible. Choux paste makes them extra light and airy, and they can be made in advance and frozen before cooking if desired. If using the salt cod recipe from the curing section of this book, cure for 24 hours and then run under cold water for about 2 hours beforehand. Shop-bought salt cod will need a 24 hour soak before use.

Serves 4 as a starter or 8 or more for canapés

350g salt cod, washed well

1 large Maris Piper potato, pricked several times with a fork

100g coarse salt

550ml milk

3 cloves garlic, crushed

1 bay leaf

1 sprig rosemary

40g cold unsalted butter, diced

50g plain flour, sifted

2 eggs, beaten

a squeeze of orange juice

2 litres vegetable oil for frying

sea salt and black pepper

For the orange alioli:

100ml alioli (see Basics)

juice of 1 orange

Preheat the oven to 220°C.

To make the orange alioli, put the orange juice in a pan and reduce to a sticky glaze. Whisk into the alioli and reserve.

Sit the potato on top of a sprinkling of coarse salt on a baking tray and bake until soft and tender. Allow to cool before peeling off the skin. Place the cod in a medium-sized saucepan and cover with the milk. Add the garlic, bay and rosemary. Bring the milk to the boil and then immediately turn off the heat. The fish will continue to cook in the residual heat before cooling down. When cool, flake into small pieces in a bowl.

To make the choux paste, bring the butter and 150ml cold water to the boil in a pan. Add the flour, stirring well until a dough forms and comes away from the sides of the pan. Remove from the heat and let cool for 5 minutes. Slowly add the eggs, beating well to make a smooth, shiny paste. Add the choux paste, cooked potato, orange juice and seasoning to the cod. Mix thoroughly. Shape into small balls or croqueta shapes. Transfer to the fridge to firm. If you wish, you can freeze them at this stage. Defrost before frying.

Heat the vegetable oil to 180°C in a deep fat fryer, or until a small piece of bread fizzles when dropped into a deep-sided pan. Fry the fritters until golden brown, cooking in batches so the oil doesn't cool down too much. Drain well on kitchen paper and serve with the alioli alongside.

A dry sherry like Fino or Manzanilla would be a good match.

CRAB SALAD

WITH QUAIL'S EGGS & GAZPACHO VINAIGRETTE

Fresh white crabmeat is a joy but needs some acidity to bring out its flavours. We pair it here with a punchy gazpacho sauce that does just that. Gazpacho is a culinary staple in Spain, thought to have originated in Andalusia. It's drunk cold in the summer months; a thirst quencher in the searing Spanish heat. Fresh crab is widely available now – ready-picked or dressed is convenient and perfectly fine. Alternatively, if you're feeling brave, ask your fishmonger to order you a live one!

Serves 4 as a starter or

6–8 as a tapa

For the gazpacho:

2 ripe plum tomatoes

½ cucumber

½ small red pepper

1 shallot

100ml extra virgin olive oil

50ml Moscatel vinegar or white balsamic vinegar

sea salt and black pepper

1 sprig basil

For the crab:

16 quail's eggs

300g white crabmeat

1 chilli, deseeded

3 spring onions

zest and juice of ½ lemon

2 teaspoons flat-leaf parsley

½ cucumber, peeled

1 teaspoon extra virgin olive oil

a few coriander shoots

sea salt and black pepper

For the gazpacho, roughly chop the tomatoes, cucumber and red pepper. Dice the shallot. Place all the gazpacho ingredients in a bowl, mix and season. Leave to marinate for 40 minutes and then transfer to a food processor and blend to a fine purée. Check the seasoning and adjust as necessary. If you prefer the gazpacho a little sharper, add a little more vinegar. If too sharp, add more olive oil. Chill the gazpacho in the fridge.

Cook the quail's eggs in boiling salted water for 3 minutes and then refresh in iced water for 2 minutes to stop the cooking process. When the eggs are cold, peel, cut in half lengthwise and set on a plate until ready to use.

Check the white crabmeat to remove any stray bits of shell that may be lurking. Finely chop the chilli, spring onions, cucumber and parsley place together with the crabmeat, lemon zest and juice in a bowl. Mix well and season to taste.

Arrange the crabmeat on serving plates, top with a few quail's eggs and spoon over the gazpacho vinaigrette. Scatter with a few coriander shoots and serve.

A coastal white from Italy or Spain, such as Albariño, would pair beautifully.

SQUID WITH SPANISH BACON

& WARM HERITAGE TOMATO SALAD

The pairing of squid with bacon is not uncommon in Spain – the flavours work very well together and the bacon fat lubricates the whole dish nicely. Try to find heritage tomatoes at a farmers' market or deli – they are at their best in the late summer months. A good selection of sweet and tart tomato varieties will create an interesting contrast of colours and flavours and make a lovely, lightly-cooked salad.

Serves 4 as a main or

6–8 as a tapa

350g fresh baby squid, cleaned and cut in half lengthwise

1 teaspoon ground cumin

1 teaspoon hot smoked paprika

375g heritage tomatoes,
select a good mix of colours
and shapes

100g broad beans, fresh or frozen

100g Spanish smoked bacon or pancetta

2 shallots, finely chopped

a squeeze of lemon juice

a small handful of mint

2 shallots, finely chopped

olive oil for cooking

sea salt and black pepper

Place the baby squid, with its tentacles, in a bowl. Add a splash of olive oil, the cumin and the paprika. Mix well, ensuring the squid is thoroughly coated, and then set aside for about 2 hours to marinate.

Meanwhile, prepare the salad ingredients. Deseed the tomatoes and dice evenly. Save the pulp for a soup or a sauce. Shell the broad beans, if fresh. If using frozen, you can either leave to defrost or blanche momentarily in boiling water. Remove any skin from the bacon, and dice into small, even pieces.

To make the 'salad', heat a frying pan over a high heat. Add a lug of oil and the bacon. Turn down the heat and cook the bacon until it's translucent. Next, add the shallots and the tomatoes, cook for a minute, and then add the broad beans. Season to taste, add a squeeze of lemon and remove from the heat.

Now for the squid. Heat a second frying pan over a high heat, add a lug of oil and then the squid. Season with salt and pepper and caramelise the squid on both sides, taking care not to overcook. This should take no more than two minutes. Spoon the warm bacon and tomato salad onto serving plates and arrange the squid on top. Scatter with roughly-torn mint, and finish with a swirl of good-quality extra virgin olive oil.

Try a Verdejo from Spain, or any good Spanish or Italian Sauvignon Blanc.

CRAB, SQUID & SAFFRON ARANCINI

WITH CHILLI ALIOLI

Hailing from 10th century Sicily, these rice balls are traditionally served cold and filled with meat ragout, though they are perfect vehicles for any type of flavouring. Here we infuse short grain rice with a saffron-rich fish stock and pack the rice balls with a variety of seafood. You could use anything you have to hand, such as prawns or small pieces of leftover fish. We serve ours hot from the fryer so the breadcrumbs are crisp and fresh. The chilli alioli on the side adds a wonderful spicy kick.

Makes about 24 arancini

500–600ml fish stock (see Basics)

2 pinches saffron threads

1 clove garlic, peeled, chopped

½ onion, finely chopped

1 teaspoon fresh chilli, chopped

100ml white wine

200g arborio rice

100g squid, chopped small

100g white crabmeat

100g tinned mussels, chopped

1 tablespoon parsley, chopped

juice of ½ lemon

olive oil for cooking

2 litres vegetable oil

2–3 eggs, beaten

80g plain flour

140g breadcrumbs

sea salt and black pepper

For the alioli:

100ml alioli (see Basics)

½ teaspoon chilli, chopped

To make the chilli alioli, simply combine the ingredients and set aside.

The rice is prepared risotto-style. Pour the fish stock into a saucepan and bring to a simmer. Add the saffron threads and simmer for a further 10 minutes to infuse the stock with flavour and turn it yellow. Heat a heavy-bottomed saucepan over a medium heat and add a lug of olive oil. Throw in the onions, garlic and chilli and cook, without colouring the ingredients, until everything is softened. Add the rice, season, and stir to coat the grains with oil. Pour in the wine and turn up the heat to reduce rapidly. Gradually ladle in the stock, stirring the rice continuously to ensure it doesn't stick. Continue this process until all the stock has been used up and the rice is al dente, which should take about 20 minutes. Add the seafood, parsley and lemon juice and stir well. Check the seasoning. The rice should be quite thick and sticky. Transfer to a tray to cool.

When cool, shape the rice into ping-pong-sized balls. Roll each ball in the flour, then in the egg and finally in the breadcrumbs. Chill the arancini in the fridge for at least an hour before frying. The arancini can be frozen at this stage if desired. Heat the vegetable oil to 170°C in a fryer or until a piece of bread turns golden brown when dropped into a deep-sided pan. Fry the arancini in batches until crisp and golden and drain on kitchen paper. Serve immediately with the chilli alioli on the side.

Try to find a Txakoli, a light sparkling white from the Basque country.

CHORIZO-STUFFED BABY SQUID

WITH SAUTÉ POTATOES, CAPERS & SAGE

Baby squid are bite-sized pockets perfect for stuffing with all manner of food and chorizo is a classic Spanish filling. Here we use a soft, semi-cured cooking chorizo with some kick. The little squid pockets are sealed with a cocktail stick and then pan-roasted. As the squid cooks, the roasting juices flavour the chorizo filling. Delicious! You could also try morcilla – the Spanish version of black pudding – or make a stuffing with garlic, parsley and breadcrumbs.

Serves 4 as a main or
6–8 as a tapa

10 cocktail sticks, cut in half, soaked in cold water

20 baby squid, cleaned, cartilage removed, tentacles removed and reserved

5–6 spicy cooking chorizo, peeled, finely chopped

3 medium King Edward potatoes, peeled, cut into 3cm dice

2 cloves garlic, skin on, crushed

15 sage leaves, roughly chopped

50g unsalted butter

25g miniature, pickled capers

zest of ½ lemon

olive oil for cooking

sea salt and black pepper

Knead the chopped chorizo in a bowl to form a rough paste. Take a piece of the paste and form into a shape to fit the squid cavity. Fill each squid to about ¾ full and press it down. Do not overfill the squids or they may burst on cooking as the chorizo expands. Secure each squid tube with a cocktail stick and reserve until ready to cook.

Cook the potatoes in salted water until tender and then drain well. Heat a non-stick sauté pan over a medium heat, add a lug of olive oil, the crushed garlic cloves and the potatoes and season well. Cook over a moderate heat, tossing occasionally to crisp and caramelise the potatoes evenly.

Meanwhile, place another non-stick pan over a moderate heat. Season the squid pockets and tentacles with salt and pepper. Add a lug of oil to the pan and add the squid. Cook for 2 minutes on each side until caramelised. Add the butter and sage and when foaming, spoon the herby butter over the squid pockets to cook further. The filling will feel firm to the touch when cooked. Now add the capers and lemon zest and remove the pan from the heat.

When the potatoes are ready, transfer to kitchen paper to drain. Arrange the squids and potatoes on serving plates and spoon over the buttery pan juices, capers and zest. Delicious with a peppery salad.

Vernaccia is a white from Sardinia which would go harmoniously with this dish.

CHARGRILLED OCTOPUS

WITH PEPERONATA

Octopus is a staple of Spanish cooking and is found all over Spain, in restaurants and domestic kitchens alike. Not so in the UK though, where it is notorious for being bland and chewy. Properly sourced and cooked, octopus is superb. At the restaurants, we use large frozen octopuses and thaw them slowly overnight. This thawing process naturally tenderizes the flesh before cooking. If you buy a fresh octopus, we recommend you freeze and then defrost it to guarantee tenderness. The sweet-and-sour pepper braise partners the rich, almost fatty, octopus incredibly well.

Serves 4 as a main or
6–8 as a tapa

1 frozen octopus, (approx. 1.5–2kg), thawed overnight in the fridge

3 bay leaves

1 onion, peeled

10 peppercorns

10 coriander seeds

For the peperonata:

5 large red peppers, quartered, seeds removed, finely sliced

2 red onions, peeled, finely sliced

2 cloves garlic, peeled, chopped

10 plum tomatoes, chopped

2 bay leaves

2 sprigs thyme

2 tablespoons demerara sugar

100ml Cabernet Sauvignon vinegar

zest and juice of 1 lemon

olive oil for cooking

sea salt and black pepper

With a sharp knife slice the head off the octopus between the tentacles and the hard, inedible mouthpiece. Discard the head. Place the octopus in a large saucepan, cover with cold water and add the bay leaves, onion, peppercorns and coriander seeds. Place the pan over a high heat and bring to the boil. Turn down to a simmer and skim off any scum or impurities that rise to the top. Cook the octopus for about 1 hour or until tender. A small, sharp knife should be able to penetrate a thick part of the octopus easily. Remove the octopus from the liquid and leave to cool. You can reserve the liquid for soups or cooking pulses.

To make the peperonata, heat a medium-sized saucepan over a high heat and add a lug of olive oil. Add the peppers, onions and garlic and cook for 20 minutes, stirring as you go. Next add the tomatoes, bay leaves, thyme, sugar and vinegar. Mix well before turning the heat down to medium. Continue to cook and stir, making sure nothing sticks. You want the tomatoes to cook down into a thick, rich sauce and the natural water to evaporate. Check for seasoning and then remove from the heat to rest. The sauce should have a rich, delicious sweet-sour flavour.

Heat a grill pan or barbecue to maximum heat. Cut the tentacles into 2 pieces each. Rub with olive oil, salt and pepper. Grill the tentacles until crisp and lightly charred. Squeeze a little lemon juice over the tentacles and serve with the peperonata.

A crisp white from Campania in Italy. Try a Falanghina or a Greco di Tufo for a fresh match.

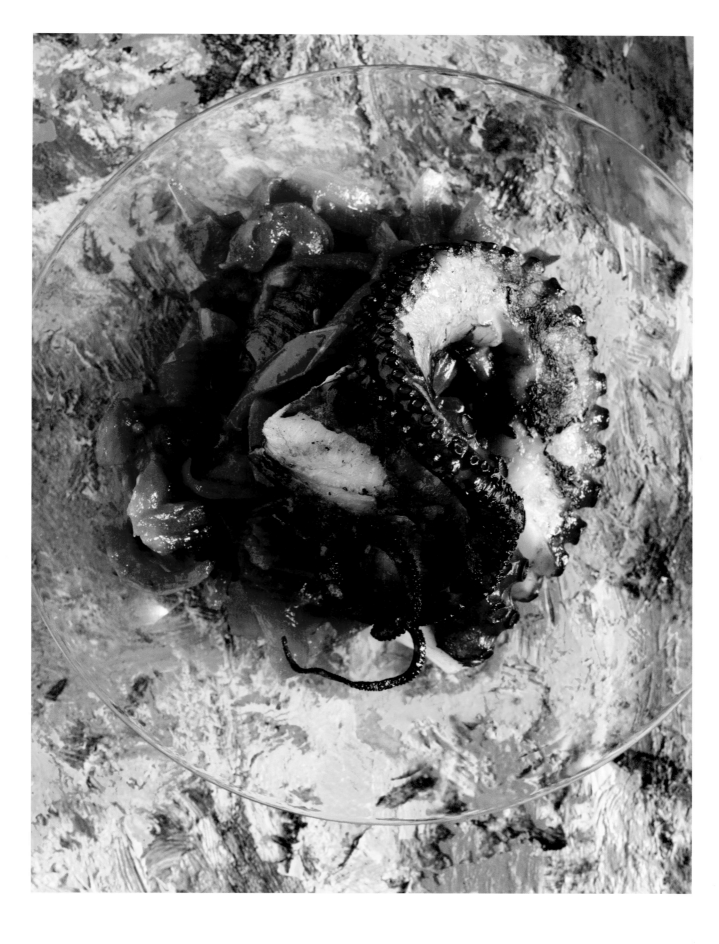

DEEP-FRIED SOFT SHELL CRAB
WITH RAISIN, PINE NUT & CAPER DRESSING

Soft shell crabs are used widely in Italy as bases for pasta sauces and in fritto misto. They look amazing when deep-fried in breadcrumbs or a light batter as the intense heat locks their natural shape. We pair the crabs with peppery wild rocket and a sweet-and-sour dressing to cut through the richness. Soft shell crabs are available frozen in Asian supermarkets or good local fishmongers. Make sure they are completely defrosted and carefully patted dry before cooking.

Serves 4 as a starter or 6–8 as a tapa

4 small soft shell crabs, defrosted, patted dry

flour for dredging

2 eggs, beaten

200g panko-style breadcrumbs

2 litres vegetable oil for deep-frying

a handful of wild rocket

sea salt and black pepper

For the dressing:

100ml extra virgin olive oil

4 tablespoons Moscatel vinegar or white balsamic vinegar

3 tablespoons raisins

3 tablespoons toasted pine nuts

3 tablespoons miniature capers

zest of 1 lemon

2 sprigs oregano, leaves picked

To make the dressing, whisk together the olive oil and vinegar and then add the raisins, pine nuts, capers and lemon zest. Season to taste and then stir in the oregano.

Pour the vegetable oil into a deep-sided pan and heat to 180°C or until a piece of bread browns quickly when dropped in.

Place the flour, beaten eggs and breadcrumbs in 3 separate bowls. Dredge the crabs in the flour and shake off any excess. Dip the crabs into the beaten egg and then coat them in the panko crumb. Carefully lower the crabs into the oil and fry for 3–4 minutes or until golden brown and crispy. Remove from the oil. Drain well and season with salt and pepper.

Season the rocket and dress with a little of the vinaigrette. Serve the crabs with the remainder of the dressing spooned over, the rocket on the side and a wedge of lemon.

A rich white from Sicily like oak-aged Fiano would be a lovely match.

Pan-Roasted Cod

With Sea Purslane, Brown Shrimps & Wild Asparagus

All our cod comes from sustainable sources. If sustainable cod isn't available, we use pollack instead which is a great substitute. Always check with your fishmonger, if you're unsure about the sustainability of fish. Good supermarkets should also be able to give you all the information you need. We source our sea purslane and wild asparagus from a forager. You may be able to find these in farmers' markets or you might know – or be! – a forager yourself. Otherwise, replace the wild asparagus with regular English asparagus and the purslane with some salty samphire.

Serves 4 as a main or

6–8 as a tapa

4 x 150g cod fillets (smaller for a tapa), skin on, scales removed

2 tablespoons plain flour

a pinch of baking powder

150ml sparkling water

125g unsalted butter, diced

100g brown shrimps

2 teaspoons miniature capers, chopped

1 teaspoon flat-leaf parsley, chopped

75g sea purslane or samphire, woody stalks removed

a squeeze of lemon

75g wild asparagus or 6 spears English asparagus, trimmed, cut into strips

olive oil for cooking

vegetable oil for frying

sea salt and black pepper

First whisk the flour, water and baking powder together to form a light batter. Rest for 10 minutes before use.

Heat the vegetable oil to 180°C in a deep fat fryer or until a piece of bread browns quickly when dropped into a high-sided pan. This is in readiness for the asparagus which you will fry once the fish is cooked.

Heat a large non-stick sauté pan over a high heat and add a lug of olive oil. Season the cod fillets on both sides and then place in the pan, skin-side down. Cook for 2–3 minutes until the skin turns golden brown and crisp. Turn the fish over and cook for a further 2 minutes to caramelise the underside. Now add the butter and cook until the butter starts to turn a light, nutty brown colour: a beurre noisette. At this stage, add the shrimps, capers, parsley, sea purslane or samphire along with a good squeeze of lemon. Season well. Warm everything through for a minute and then turn off the heat. Check the cod is cooked by inserting a cocktail stick into a fleshy part – there shouldn't be any resistance.

Now the asparagus. Dip the spears into the batter and carefully fry in batches. When golden brown, transfer to kitchen paper to drain and season well. Arrange the cod fillets on serving plates and spoon over the delicious, buttery juices and the shrimps. Drizzle some juices around the fish as well and top with the crispy asparagus.

A white from Majorca will be a great match; ideally one from Binissalem DOC.

STEAMED SEA BREAM

WITH BRAISED FENNEL & LEMON CONDIMENT

It's rare to find steamed fish on menus nowadays – everyone's pan-roasting or chargrilling – but there's something very fresh and natural about cooking fish in this manner. Only use supremely fresh fish when steaming and nothing too meaty, as you want the fish to cook quickly without taking on too much moisture. Sea bream works brilliantly and is a tasty, economical fish, now widely available. The farmed variety is very good and available year-round, while the wild variety, in particular Cornish, has a stronger, sweeter flavour and lovely pink flesh.

Serves 4 as a main or

6–8 as a tapa

You will need a large steamer

For the fish:

4 fillets sea bream

2 medium heads of fennel, trimmed, quartered

1 glass dry white wine

1 small red chilli, deseeded, chopped

2 sprigs thyme

500ml fish stock (see Basics)

olive oil

sea salt and black pepper

For the lemon condiment:

3 unwaxed lemons, each cut into 8, seeds removed

3 tablespoons caster sugar

100ml extra virgin olive oil

2 tablespoon marjoram or oregano leaves

First make the lemon condiment. Blend the lemons and sugar in a food processor until the lemons break down to a coarse consistency, but not a purée. Now gradually pour in the olive oil, pulsing at the same time, so that the lemons emulsify with the oil. Season and stir in the marjoram or oregano. You should end up with a viscous, jam-like consistency.

Heat a medium-sized saucepan over a medium heat and add a lug of olive oil. Throw in the fennel quarters, season with salt and pepper and lightly sauté on all sides to brown. Now pour in the wine, add the chilli and thyme sprigs and turn the heat up to maximum. When the wine has come to the boil, reduce it rapidly until a glaze is achieved and then add the fish stock. Bring the fish stock to the boil, turn the heat down to a simmer and place a lid on the pan. Cook the fennel until tender and the fish stock has reduced to sauce consistency.

A few minutes before the fennel is ready, set up your steamer and bring the water to the boil over a high heat. Season the bream fillets with salt and pepper, place in the top of the steamer and cook until the fish is opaque or just cooked. Transfer the bream to serving plates. Divide out the fennel and spoon over the braising liquor. Serve with the lemon condiment on the side.

A delicate white from Northern Italy would work. Try a Gavi di Gavi, or if you can find it, Pigato.

PAN-ROASTED SEA TROUT

WITH COURGETTES, PARSLEY-CRUSTED CLAMS & CHILLI

Sea trout's in season in early summer and the British coastal variety's the best available. We love it for its versatility: it can be served raw, semi-cured, pan-roasted or steamed. It has all the qualities of salmon but with a leaner flesh and a more pronounced flavour. Here we roast it with the skin on for texture and flavour and serve it medium so the flesh is beautifully moist. If your fishmonger can't find sea trout, then a decent organic salmon would be fine. The clams could be replaced with mussels.

Serves 4 as a main or
6–8 as a tapa or starter

4 x 200g sea trout fillets
(cut smaller for tapas), skin intact

2 handfuls clams, such as
Parloude or Venus, washed under
cold running water for a few
minutes and drained

2 slices stale white bread,
crusts removed

1 large handful flat-leaf parsley

1 clove garlic, peeled, chopped

1 small glass white wine

2 medium green courgettes, sliced
into rounds

1 small red chilli, cut in half,
deseeded

olive oil for cooking

good extra virgin olive oil

sea salt and black pepper

Preheat the grill to medium. Heat a saucepan over a high heat and add the clams and the wine. Place a lid on the pan and shake. Steam until the clams have opened, then remove from the pan to cool. Discard any clams that are still closed. Now make the parsley crumbs by placing the bread, garlic and parsley in a food processor and pulsing until everything has combined. Add a good lug of olive oil and blend further until you achieve a fine crumb. Season well. Spoon some of the parsley crumb on top of the clam meat in each shell. You should slightly mound it so you have a good crust-to-clam ratio. Place the crusted clams on a grill tray, but do not cook yet.

Meanwhile, toss the courgettes in a bowl with some olive oil, salt and pepper. Heat a large sauté pan over a medium heat, add the courgettes, stir and lower the heat. Cook the courgettes until lightly coloured and tender. Finely slice the chilli and add to the courgettes. When cooked, remove the courgettes from the pan and keep warm.

Heat a non-stick sauté pan over a high heat and add a lug of olive oil. Season the trout and place skin-side down in the pan. Turn the heat down to medium and press the fillets gently into the pan. Cook the trout until crisp and brown and then turn over to finish cooking – about 6 minutes in all. A minute before the trout is ready, place the clams under the grill. Cook until the crust turns light brown and crisp. Transfer the courgettes onto plates and top with the trout. Arrange the clams around the courgettes.

To be different, try a light red, like a Pinot Noir.

ROASTED SCALLOPS

WITH SQUASH PURÉE, MIGAS & TRUFFLE DRESSING

At the restaurants we serve our scallops in their shells as they look so attractive. A good fish-monger will be able to obtain hand-dived scallops in the shell and shuck them for you. Ask to keep the shells to use as scallop-serving receptacles! Cornish or Scottish hand-dived scallops are among the best in the world and are caught sustainably, or you can also buy good-quality farmed scallops accredited by the Marine Stewardship Council. The truffle dressing and sweetness of the squash work beautifully with the scallops.

Serves 4 as a starter or light main or 6 as a tapa

12 medium hand-dived scallops or good-quality farmed scallops (shells reserved if you have them)

1 butternut squash, peeled, diced

olive oil for cooking

1 clove garlic, crushed

1 sprig thyme

2 tablespoons dried breadcrumbs

For the truffle dressing:

2 banana shallots, peeled, finely chopped

knob of unsalted butter

extra virgin olive oil

1 teaspoon Moscatel vinegar or white balsamic vinegar

1 tablespoon white truffle oil

sea salt and black pepper

Preheat the oven to 190°C.

Place the diced squash on a baking tray, drizzle with olive oil and season. Cook in the oven until the squash is lightly caramelised, soft and tender. While still hot, transfer the squash to a blender or food processor and blend to a smooth purée. You may need to add a little water to assist the puréeing process.

To make the migas, heat a sauté pan over a medium heat and add a lug of olive oil. Add the garlic and thyme and then the breadcrumbs. Season well. Stir constantly until the breadcrumbs are crisp and golden. As soon as they are done, transfer onto kitchen paper to drain. Put all the ingredients for the truffle dressing, except the truffle oil, in a small saucepan and place over a low heat. Cook very slowly until the shallots are soft and have almost melted into the butter. Remove from the heat and cool down before adding the truffle oil and seasoning.

Heat a large sauté pan over a high heat and add a lug of olive oil. Season the scallops and place in the pan. Cook on one side until caramelised and a crust has formed and then flip over to cook for another 2 minutes until the scallops are just cooked through. They should have a little spring in them when prodded. Serve the scallops in the shells, if you have them, with a little purée underneath and some truffle dressing and breadcrumbs spooned on top.

Godello, from Galicia, is a white variety that matches well with this dish.

BRAISED HAKE

WITH MUSSELS, CHORIZO & OLIVE OIL MASH

Cooking fish on the bone has fallen from favour recently which is a shame as the bone flavours the fish beautifully and, when braised as in this recipe, the natural gelatin in the bone adds body to the sauce. Hake is a classic Spanish white fish, associated with many of Spain's regional fish dishes. This meaty, flavoursome fish is gradually creeping onto the radar of British chefs and foodies alike and is well worth a try. Cod or pollack would also work well here.

**Serves 4 as a main or
6–8 as a tapa**

4 x 180g hake steaks, bone in

150g hot cooking chorizo, peeled, diced (about 3 sausages)

1 small banana shallot, peeled, diced

24 mussels, washed well

100ml medium dry sherry

100ml white wine

30g unsalted butter

1 tablespoon flat-leaf parsley, chopped

a squeeze of lemon

olive oil for cooking

sea salt and black pepper

For the mash:

2 large Désirée potatoes, peeled, evenly diced

20g unsalted butter

120ml double cream

75ml extra virgin olive oil, preferably Arbequina

Place the potatoes in a pan of salted water and bring to the boil. Simmer until the potatoes are tender. Drain well and mash until very smooth. Return the mash to the pan over a low heat and stir in the butter and cream. Season the potatoes well and then slowly whisk in the olive oil until incorporated.

Heat a non-stick pan over a high heat and add a lug of olive oil. Season the hake and place in the pan. Sear on one side for 2 minutes. Turn the fish over and add the chorizo, shallots and mussels. Cook for a further minute or 2, until the chorizo has started to release its oil and the mussels have started to open. Drain off a little of the oil, and then add the sherry and wine. Bring the liquids to the boil and reduce steadily. After 2–3 minutes turn the hake again and then add the butter and parsley. Stir, making sure the butter and wines have combined well. Scrape any sediment from the bottom of the pan to flavour the sauce, which should achieve a syrupy consistency. Check that the hake is cooked through by pushing a small knife in near the bone: the fish will be opaque when done. Check the sauce for seasoning and add a squeeze of lemon juice.

Spoon the mash onto serving plates and top with the hake, chorizo and mussels. Pour over the sauce.

A rosé will work wonders with this; try full-bodied from Tuscany or lighter from Northern Italy.

PAN-FRIED GURNARD

WITH SPROUTING BROCCOLI, JERSEY ROYALS, PANCETTA & BLOOD ORANGE

This lovely, light, early spring dish is a delight and makes use of the abundance of produce available at that time of year: colourful blood oranges, sweet, nutty Jersey Royals and purple sprouting broccoli. You can omit the pancetta if you want a meat-free option, but it does add an underlying richness. Gurnard is a sustainable favourite at our restaurants, yet is much underused in general. It has a firm, meaty flesh similar to haddock and a strong, pronounced flavour. It's delicious and can stand up to big Mediterranean flavours.

**Serves 4 as a main or
6–8 as a starter or tapa**

4 red gurnard fillets, skin on

200g purple sprouting broccoli, trimmed, woody stalks removed

20 small Jersey Royals, cut in half

80g smoked pancetta, diced

juice of 1 blood orange

2 small blood oranges, segmented

4 tablespoons good-quality extra virgin olive oil

sherry vinegar or Moscatel vinegar to taste

olive oil for cooking

sea salt and black pepper

Blanche the broccoli in boiling salted water for a few minutes until just cooked. Refresh in cold water to keep the colour, drain well and reserve in a bowl. Place the potatoes in a pan of salted water, bring to the boil and cook until just tender. Drain.

Place a non-stick sauté pan over a medium heat and add a good lug of olive oil. Add the potatoes, cut-side down, along with the pancetta. Cook until the pancetta releases its fat and the potatoes caramelise. Remove and add to the broccoli.

Season the fish fillets well and place, skin-side down, in the same pan. Cook for 2–3 minutes until the skin colours. Turn over the fish, cook for another couple of minutes and remove from the pan. Pour the orange juice into the pan and cook until sticky. Pour the juice over the broccoli, pancetta and potatoes, and then add the orange segments, extra virgin olive oil and a dash of vinegar. Season well and mix together.

Spoon the broccoli and potato salad onto individual serving plates and top with the pan-fried gurnard. Serve straight away.

Hunt down a good Soave from Veneto in Northern Italy.

MEAT

We take our meat seriously at the restaurants. It's a huge part of what we do and we work very hard with our suppliers to ensure we only use the best quality meat and that the breeding and husbandry are immaculate. Spain and Italy have strong meat-eating cultures and travelling around these countries, you get a feel for the diversity of meat cooking styles and the more unusual methods and cuts of meat that we don't generally see in the UK. The ethos of nose-to-tail eating, where nothing goes to waste, is very prominent. Offal and extremities are popular, as are lesser known cuts, such as beef onglet and bavette, lamb's belly and pork rump.

At the restaurants, we love to use the black-footed Ibérico pig from Spain. When fresh, as opposed to the more usual cured jamón Ibérico, the versatility of this product is on a par with a fine quality, mature beef. These pigs are raised in the dehesa (oak-forested pastureland) of Extremadura, where they're free to roam wild, snuffling up the constant supply of acorns that fall to the ground. The pigs' immaculate breeding heritage, their unique acorn-fed diet and the stringent selection and slaughtering process results in meat that is rich and full-flavoured. Unusually for pork, it can be cooked rare and even eaten raw. They really are the king of pigs!

Our Red Poll beef and salt marsh lamb is supplied by George at the Rare Breed Meat Company in Essex. As he breeds the cows and lambs himself, he has an in-depth understanding of the whole meat process. The animals are reared in a free-range environment, then humanely slaughtered and hung for a good length of time to allow the flavours to mature naturally and the meat to tenderise. Finally, expert butchery practices are used to produce the best cuts of meat. They also shoot their own game allowing us access to wood pigeon, venison, snipe and pheasant when in season. Meanwhile, Mark Jones has been supplying us with deliciously Old Spot pork for years. He drives down in his van twice a week from rural Wales and drops off pork bellies and other delights.

We've always enjoyed using the more economical, labour-intensive cuts. Long, slow braises, confits and pot roasts are time-consuming and require a fair amount of skill but they're worth it. There's nothing like a meltingly sticky oxtail, or a confit duck leg that's been finished in the oven to crisp its skin. Our ever popular confit Old Spot pork belly with cannellini beans has become a signature dish. The open grill also features prominently in our kitchens with its flames adding smoky caramelisation to lamb cutlets, ribeyes and Ibérico pork steaks.

The recipes here range from the quick and simple to the labour-intensive and time-consuming, so do check this out before embarking on a long recipe when you want to eat in twenty minutes! Some of the more unusual cuts will need to be ordered in advance from your butcher, who will be able to advise you on cooking times and give you information on the best breeds.

GRILLED PRESA

WITH CAPERS, SHALLOTS, LEMON & SHERRY

This simple tapa pairs smoky grilled Ibérico presa (pork shoulder) with a rich, tangy sherry jus; flavours which complement each other perfectly. In the summer, try cooking the presa over coals on a barbecue to bring out its fantastic flavour. An open flame does wonderful things to meat. The elements of the sauce can be simplified into a vinaigrette, if you like. Just take out the sherry and stock reduction, and replace with a basic vinaigrette recipe.

Serves 4 as a main or
6–8 as a tapa

700g Ibérico presa, cut into
4 steaks

100ml Manzanilla sherry

600ml dark chicken stock
(see Basics)

knob of unsalted butter

2 banana shallots, finely diced

10 lemon segments

1½ tablespoons capers, chopped

3 teaspoons parsley, chopped

olive oil for cooking

sea salt and black pepper

Heat a grill pan or barbecue to medium heat.

Season the presa with salt and pepper and rub with olive oil. Place on the grill and cook for 2–3 minutes on each side or until the meat is nicely charred and cooked to medium rare. The meat will give a little spring when prodded with a finger. Rest in a warm spot for a few minutes before slicing.

Heat a small saucepan over a high heat and add the sherry. Reduce until syrupy and then add the stock. Bring to the boil and then reduce by half. Whisk in the butter and add the shallots, lemon, capers and parsley. Season to taste and keep warm. Any juices that have run from the meat while resting can be added to the sauce for flavour.

Carve the presa into thin slices and arrange on serving plates. Spoon over the sauce, garnish with some fresh micro herbs, such as cress, if you like, and serve.

For a great match, and a challenge, try to find a Mencia wine from Bierzo, Spain.

MINI IBÉRICO PORK BURGER

When we opened Opera Tavern in 2011 this burger was an instant hit. Regular customers have even been known to compete to see who can eat the most! It's an Iberian version of the classic burger, made luxurious by the addition of foie gras and melted Manchego cheese. Pork shoulder is the best cut as the fat-to-meat ratio is just right for a succulent burger. You could use a good-quality, rare breed pork mince instead of Ibérico pork, but will need to make sure you cook the burger until it's well done.

Makes 8 small burgers

600g Ibérico pork shoulder mince

2 tablespoons milk

2 shallots, finely chopped, sweated in olive oil

2 tablespoons breadcrumbs

40g foie gras, either buy frozen or freeze for ease of grating

1 red onion, cut into fine rings

milk

sweet smoked paprika

flour for dusting

50g aged Manchego cheese, grated

8 x 8cm burger buns, cut in half

2 tablespoons alioli (see Basics)

8 small lettuce leaves

3 tablespoons red onion marmalade (see Basics)

8 guindilla peppers to garnish

olive oil for cooking

sea salt and black pepper

Mix the Ibérico pork with the milk, breadcrumbs, shallots and season with salt and pepper. Quickly grate in the frozen foie gras and mix again. Shape into eight patties and chill in the fridge for at least an hour.

Soak the onion rings in milk and drain well. Dredge the onions in a mixture made of equal quantities of smoked paprika and flour. Heat some olive oil in a pan and shallow fry the onion rings until crisp and golden brown. Drain well and season.

Drizzle some olive oil onto both sides of the burger and season. Grill or fry for 3 minutes on either side until nicely browned and still pink in the centre. Rest the burger for a minute or so in a warm spot and sprinkle on some grated manchego. It will melt slowly over the burger. Grill the burger bun on both sides until lightly charred.

To assemble the burger, spoon some alioli onto the base of the burger bun. Top with a lettuce leaf, a dollop of the onion marmalade, the burger, 2 crispy onion rings and finally the top of the burger bun. Slide a small wooden skewer or toothpick through the middle of the burger to secure everything in place. Serve with the guindilla peppers on the side.

A Spanish or Italian lager: Cruz Campo or Birra Moretti.

IBÉRICO PORK TARTARE

WITH QUAIL'S EGG

This dish shows the true versatility of Ibérico pork. It's a classic tartare with the rich Ibérico pork treated in the same way as beef. The addition of lemon zest, chilli and marjoram adds Mediterranean zing and the little egg yolk is perfect for tapas-sized portions. At the restaurants, we cut and season the meat to order, which is the only way to prepare tartare. How you like your tartare is highly subjective: it's all about the seasoning. The quantities given here are meant as a guide only.

Serves 6–8 as a starter or tapa

300g Ibérico pork loin, trimmed of fat

1 small shallot, finely chopped

1 small red chilli, deseeded, finely diced

zest of 1 lemon

1 tablespoon capers, chopped

1 teaspoon Dijon mustard (or to taste)

a splash of Cabernet Sauvignon vinegar (to taste)

4 quail's eggs, separated, yolks retained

1 teaspoon marjoram leaves

extra virgin olive oil

sea salt and black pepper

Using a very sharp knife, finely dice the pork and place in a mixing bowl. Add the shallot, chilli, lemon zest, capers and mustard. Season well and mix thoroughly. Add a few splashes of olive oil and vinegar. Mix again and taste. You're aiming for a punchy acidity but not so punchy that it overpowers the flavour of the pork. When you're happy with the flavours, spoon the tartare onto plates and shape into attractively presented mounds.

Top each of the mounds with a quail's egg yolk and finish with a sprinkling of sea salt, pepper and fresh marjoram leaves. Serve the tartare with ciabatta croutons.

Oak-aged white from Northern Italy or white Rioja.

IBÉRICO PORK CARPACCIO

WITH WILD MUSHROOMS, TRUFFLE ALIOLI & WOOD SORREL

This twist on the classic beef carpaccio makes a great dinner party dish – simple but impressive. You can prepare the plates of pork carpaccio in advance and simply finish with seasoning before you serve. Any meaty, flavoursome mushrooms would work here – porcini, morels and girolles all have their seasons so you can vary the dish according to the time of year. Wood sorrel is a tiny, foraged leaf that has an intense, citrusy flavour. If your greengrocer can't source it for you, then some shredded sorrel or rocket leaves would suffice.

Serves 6–8 as a starter or tapa

1kg Ibérico pork loin, trimmed of fat

1 small bunch of flat-leaf parsley, finely chopped

3 tablespoons Dijon mustard

500g wild mushrooms such as porcini, morels or girolles, trimmed, washed, cut into small pieces

2 tablespoons Moscatel vinegar or white balsamic vinegar

4 tablespoons extra virgin olive oil

5 tablespoons alioli (see Basics mixed with 1 tablespoon white truffle oil

1 teaspoon spring or summer truffle, finely grated (optional)

small handful wood sorrel or sorrel leaves, shredded

olive oil for cooking

sea salt and black pepper

Place a large sauté pan over a high heat and add a lug of olive oil. Season the loin well with salt and pepper. When the oil starts to smoke, put the loin in the pan and seal on all sides until nicely caramelised, which should take approximately 2 minutes per side. Once the pork is entirely sealed, remove from the pan and allow to cool. Once cool, smear the loin with the mustard. Roll the pork in the chopped parsley, pressing the parsley firmly into the sides of the meat to ensure a good, even coating. Measure out 3 lengths of cling film long enough to wrap the pork in and place them one on top of the other. Sit the pork on top of the cling film layers, positioning it slightly to the bottom. Wrap the cling film very tightly around the pork – rather like rolling a cigarette – until the pork is sealed. Fold the ends around the pork and transfer to the fridge for an hour.

Heat a sauté pan over a high heat and add a lug of olive oil. When the oil is hot, add the mushrooms and season well. Sauté quickly until caramelised and just cooked. Transfer the mushrooms to a bowl, add the vinegar and extra virgin olive oil and mix well.

Take a sharp knife and carefully slice the pork, still wrapped in cling film, into thin rounds. Remove the cling film from the pork and arrange the slices on serving plates. When ready to serve, sprinkle the carpaccio with sea salt and spoon over the mushrooms, vinaigrette and truffle alioli. Finish with a scattering of sorrel, and truffle if using.

A sherry, such as an Amontillado or Oloroso.

Confit Of Pork Belly

With Rosemary Cannellini Beans

A Salt Yard classic, this dish looks deceptively simple with just two elements – pork and beans. The skill lies in sourcing excellent pork and the lengthy preparation process. We use Gloucester Old Spot as it has the perfect meat-to-fat ratio and great depth of flavour. There are three steps in preparing the pork. Firstly, we add flavour and reduce moisture by salting overnight; next, we slow-cook in duck fat until the pork is tender; and finally, just before serving, we fast-roast the pork skin-side down to achieve the best crackling you've ever had.

Serves 4 as a main or

6–8 as a tapa

For the pork:

1.5kg rare breed (preferably Old Spot) pork belly, skin intact, ribs removed

½ bunch rosemary, leaves picked

6 cloves garlic, crushed

750g coarse sea salt

2 litres duck fat, slowly melted

vegetable oil for cooking

For the beans:

200g dried cannellini beans, soaked overnight

200g unsalted butter

4 sprigs rosemary, leaves finely chopped

sea salt and black pepper

Note: you will need to work a day ahead for this recipe!

Place the pork belly skin-side up on a board and take a very sharp knife to score through the skin. Make several cuts at a 45 degree angle and then repeat in the opposite direction. Be careful not to cut too deeply into the flesh: you just want to pierce the skin but no further. Now sprinkle half the salt, rosemary and garlic on the bottom of a tray and place the pork on top. Add the rest of the salt, rosemary and garlic and rub in evenly. Cover the tray with cling film and transfer to the fridge for about 12 hours.

After the 12 hours is up, preheat the oven to 170°C. Remove the pork from the fridge and rinse off the salt marinade under cold, running water for 5 minutes or so until all the salt is removed. Dry the pork well on kitchen paper.

Place the pork in a deep-sided tray and pour over the melted duck fat so the pork is just covered. Place a plate on top to keep the pork submerged and then cover the tray with aluminium foil. Place the pork in the oven and cook for 40 minutes or until the fat starts to slowly bubble.

Turn down the heat to 120°C and cook for a further 1.5 hours or until the pork is very tender and a knife will go through it like butter. During this part of the confit process, the heat of the fat must be consistently low, otherwise the pork will start to fry and toughen up in the fat. The pork should not caramelise at all but just bubble slowly in the fat. When the pork is cooked, carefully remove it from the fat and drain well. Place the pork skin-side down on a tray and

place another tray on top. Weigh this tray down with some tins or other weights and place in a cool area. When cool, transfer to the fridge and leave until completely cold. The weights will ensure the pork is of an even thickness and that the skin is flat for roasting. While the pork is cooling cook the beans in boiling, unsalted water until tender.

When ready to roast, preheat the oven to 220°C. Remove the pork from the fridge and cut into 4 pieces. Place skin side-down in the tray and roast for 12–15 minutes, or until the pork is hot and the skin is a mahogany colour and beautifully crisp. Meanwhile, place the cooked beans, butter and rosemary in 200ml of water in a saucepan and bring to the boil, then lower to a simmer and season well. Ladle the beans onto plates, top with a piece of pork belly and serve.

Full-bodied old vine Garnacha from Spain.

GRILLED CHORIZO

WITH MARINATED PEPPERS & BASIL

The combination of hot, spicy chorizo straight from the grill and cool, sweet peppers is an instant classic. You'll need cooking (or parilla) chorizo for this recipe. It's been semi-cured but needs to be further cooked unlike the chorizo you get on a charcuterie board. We've always bought our chorizo from Brindisa and think it's the best, but any good-quality deli or supermarket chorizo will do. Fragrant basil torn on top of the chorizo adds a great final note. If you feel like an earthier flavour, try marjoram or oregano instead.

Serves 4 as a main or 6–8 as a tapa

600g picante (spicy) cooking chorizo, peeled
(approx. 6 sausages)

3 large red peppers

2 large yellow peppers

100ml extra virgin olive oil

100ml Moscatel vinegar or white balsamic vinegar

3 cloves garlic, crushed

large handful fresh basil leaves

sea salt and black pepper

Preheat the barbecue or a grill pan to a high heat.

Place the peppers on the grill and blister on all sides until cooked. Transfer to a bowl, cover with cling film and leave to steam for 5 minutes. This will help the skins slip off more easily. Turn the grill down to medium heat.

Remove the peppers from the bowl and ease off the skins. Break the peppers open and remove the seeds and white ribs from inside, making sure no seeds remain. Cut into thin strips and place in a clean bowl. Add the oil and vinegar and season well. Mix in the crushed garlic.

Cut the chorizo sausages in half lengthwise. Place on the grill and cook for 2 minutes or so on either side until lightly charred and cooked through. The chorizo will be firm to the touch when ready. Remove from the grill and drain well on kitchen paper.

Arrange the peppers on rustic-style terracotta dishes or similar and top with the hot chorizo. Scatter with torn basil leaves and serve immediately.

A red with spice: Syrah, Merlot or Bobal from Spain.

Braised Pigs' Cheeks

With Dry Cider, Fresh Peas, Pancetta & Pan-Fried Apple

Pig's cheeks are a delicacy in Spain and Italy, revered for their incredibly tasty flesh and unctuous, sticky texture. You have to cook them for a couple of hours to get the meat really soft but they're completely worth the wait. Your butcher will be happy to supply you with these as they're relatively underused in the UK and often go to waste. We like to serve pigs' cheeks year-round, not just in the colder months. Although the cheeks are richly braised here, this dish is made lighter by the bright, summery flavours of the apples, pancetta and peas.

Serves 4 as a main or
6–8 as a tapa

8 pigs' cheeks, trimmed of fat, ask your butcher for the 'spots' not the whole jowl

1 large carrot

1 small onion

1 stick celery

2 bay leaves

½ head garlic

250ml dry cider

1–1.25 litres dark chicken stock, enough to cover the cheeks (see Basics)

120g pancetta or smoked bacon, cut into lardons

1 Braeburn apple, peeled, cored, cut into 12 slices

400g peas, fresh or frozen

40g unsalted butter, diced

2 sprigs oregano, leaves picked

olive oil for cooking

sea salt and black pepper

Preheat the oven to 160°C.

Peel and roughly chop the carrot, onion and celery. Heat a large ovenproof casserole pan over a medium heat and add a lug of olive oil. Add the cheeks and colour for 3 minutes on each side to caramelise and create a nice crust. This process is very important and will add layers of flavour to the finished dish. When the meat is well-coloured, add the carrots, onion, celery, bay and garlic and stir well to coat with the oil. Cook the vegetables for approximately 5 minutes to achieve a good colour. Next, pour in the cider and bring to the boil. Reduce the cider until it's nearly evaporated and the alcohol has burnt away. Now add the chicken stock and again, bring to the boil and then turn down the heat so you have a slow simmer. Skim off the scum that forms on the surface of the stock with a ladle.

Cover the top of the casserole with a lid and place in the oven for approximately 2 hours, or until the cheeks are meltingly tender and the stock has reduced to a rich, thick gravy. Have a peek under the lid every so often to see how things are doing. 30 minutes before the cheeks are ready, take the lid off to let the stock evaporate and reduce more quickly.

20 minutes before the cheeks are ready, heat a large sauté pan to a high heat and add a lug of olive oil. Throw in the lardons and cook briskly to colour lightly and release their fat. Next add the apple slices and colour on both sides. Add the peas and butter and turn the heat down to low. Season with salt and pepper and simmer slowly until the

peas are cooked. At this point, add a splash of water and the oregano leaves. Lightly crush some of the peas with the back of a fork to create some texture. Check you're happy with the seasoning.

When done, remove the cheeks from the oven and check the sauce has reduced to a thick gravy. If still a little thin, transfer the casserole onto the stove top and heat briskly over a high heat to reduce the sauce. Divide the apples, peas and pancetta between plates and then spoon the cheeks, vegetables and sauce from the casserole on top. Serve. This dish is lovely with some creamy Parmesan-rich polenta to soak up the juices.

Tip: Never season a braise before or during cooking, as you can never tell how its taste will develop over the long cooking process. Generally, it will be very full-flavoured and not need any additional seasoning.

A rich, rustic red from Umbria, Italy. Try a Sagrantino de Montefalco.

GRILLED CHICKEN

WITH TRUFFLED MACARONI & ASPARAGUS

We use chicken thigh for this recipe as it has so much flavour and stays nice and juicy when grilled or barbecued. The truffled macaroni is a revelation. A simple workhorse pasta given a special treatment of truffle and chicken velouté (reduced chicken stock and cream), this is comfort food at its most luxurious. Asparagus in season is great, or you could use peas, broad beans or spinach.

Serves 4 as a main or

6–8 as a tapa

4 large free-range chicken thighs, skin intact

2 litres dark chicken stock (see Basics)

250ml double cream

1 tablespoon truffle oil

2 shallots, peeled, finely chopped

1 clove garlic, finely chopped

320g short macaroni/tubetti

100g chestnut mushrooms, finely sliced

12 asparagus spears, trimmed, and sliced in half

1 small seasonal black truffle (optional)

olive oil for cooking

sea salt and black pepper

To make the velouté, place 1 litre of the chicken stock in a saucepan and reduce slowly by two-thirds over a medium heat. Add the cream and reduce by half. Season with salt and pepper and then stir in the truffle oil.

Heat the remaining chicken stock in a small saucepan over a low heat and keep on a slow simmer until required. Meanwhile, in a medium-sized saucepan over a moderate heat, cook the shallots and garlic in a lug of olive oil for 2–3 minutes without colouring. Add the pasta and stir well, coating it with the shallots and the oil. Season well. Gradually add the hot chicken stock, a ladle at a time, stirring as you go. This is a similar process to cooking risotto – the pasta will cook slowly, absorbing the stock. When all the chicken stock has been incorporated, the pasta will be three-quarters cooked. Turn down the heat and add the chicken and truffle velouté to the pasta. Stir well and then continue to cook for 4–5 minutes until the pasta is al dente and the sauce has reduced to a thick, creamy consistency. It should have the consistency of risotto: not too wet, but still with some movement.

Heat a grill pan or barbecue to maximum heat. Season the chicken thighs and drizzle with olive oil. Place on the grill, skin-side down, and cook until the skin has crisped and charred. Then turn the heat down and turn over the chicken. Continue to cook for another 6–7 minutes or until the thighs are cooked through and the juices run clear. Rest in a warm spot. While the chicken is cooking, heat a sauté pan over a medium heat and add a lug of olive oil. Add the mushrooms and quickly fry until browned and

cooked through. Add these to the pasta. Add the asparagus to the same pan and cook for 3–4 minutes or until just tender. Season well.

Check the final seasoning of the pasta and give a final stir. Divide the pasta between serving bowls and top with the asparagus and then the grilled chicken. Shave or grate over the truffle, if using.

A full-bodied white from Spain, something from Rueda or Priorat.

MARINATED RABBIT
WITH SPRING ONIONS, MORCILLA & MOJO VERDE

Rabbit is not that common in the UK but it's widely used on the Continent, where it's held in almost as high esteem as chicken. It's a delicious, healthy meat and incredibly versatile. You'll probably have to order it from the butcher, as it's rarely seen on supermarket shelves. Ask for farmed rabbit. Wild rabbit is also delicious but suits longer, slower cooking techniques. Farmed rabbit is very lean so we add a rich, fatty Spanish-style black pudding to this recipe and finish the dish with a punchy salsa from the Canary Islands called mojo verde.

Serves 4 as a main or
6–8 as a tapa

2 rabbit saddles, boned and rolled

5 sprigs thyme

500ml white wine

zest of ½ lemon

100ml extra virgin olive oil

4 cloves garlic, peeled, crushed

2 bunches spring onions, trimmed at both ends

30g unsalted butter

300g Spanish morcilla or black pudding, skinned, sliced

olive oil for cooking

sea salt and black pepper

For the mojo verde:

½ bunch flat-leaf parsley leaves

½ bunch coriander leaves

½ bunch mint leaves

4 salted anchovies

3 tablespoons Moscatel vinegar or white balsamic vinegar

5 tablespoons extra virgin olive oil

Place the rabbit saddles in a container with the thyme, wine, lemon zest, olive oil and garlic, and leave to marinate for a couple of hours. Meanwhile make the mojo verde. Place all the ingredients in a food processor, blitz the herbs until you have a smooth purée, season with salt and pepper and set aside. The last bit of preparation is bringing a pan of salted water to the boil and blanching the spring onions until just cooked. Drain and reserve.

When ready to cook, remove the saddles from the marinade and season well with salt and pepper. Heat a sauté pan over a medium heat and add a lug of olive oil. Place the rabbit saddles in the pan and cook for 2 minutes on each side, ensuring the rabbit is nicely caramelised. Now add the spring onions to the pan and season with salt and pepper. Sauté the onions for a minute or so to add some colour, then turn the heat down to low and add the butter. Continue to cook the rabbit, turning occasionally, for 3–4 minutes until just cooked through or medium. Press the saddle: there should be a little spring in the flesh when ready. Remove the rabbit and spring onions from the pan and rest in a warm spot. Add the morcilla slices to the pan and turn the heat back up to moderate. Cook the morcilla for 2 minutes on each side and then transfer to kitchen paper to drain.

Slice the rabbit into chunks and arrange on serving plates with the morcilla and spring onions. Spoon over the mojo verde and serve.

A hearty Spanish red from the island of Majorca.

CHARGRILLED LAMB CHOPS
WITH FRESH PEAS, BROAD BEANS, ASPARAGUS & MINT ALIOLI

Smoky, hot-off-the barbecue lamb chops are served here with spring vegetables and dressed with a punchy, garlic-infused vinaigrette. Mint alioli on the side finishes the dish beautifully. We use salt marsh lamb when available as it has very tender flesh and an interesting, slightly briny flavour with some floral notes. Your butcher should be able to source it for you. If not, you could try getting hold of some hogget (one-year-old sheep) which has a more pronounced flavour and meatier texture.

**Serves 4 as a main or
6–8 as a tapa**

8 lamb chops, about 120g each

4 mint stalks

4 cloves garlic, peeled, finely sliced

75ml extra virgin olive oil

4 tablespoons Moscatel vinegar or white balsamic vinegar

150g peas, fresh or frozen

50g broad beans, fresh or frozen, shelled

12 spears of asparagus, trimmed and peeled, if necessary

handful mint leaves, roughly chopped

olive oil for cooking

100ml alioli (see Basics) mixed with 1 tablespoon chopped fresh mint leaves

sea salt and black pepper

Preheat a grill pan or barbecue to maximum.

Heat the extra virgin olive oil, the mint stalks and the sliced garlic in a small saucepan over a medium heat. When the garlic starts to turn golden, add the vinegar and season with salt and pepper. Remove the pan from the heat and allow the oil to infuse for a few minutes, before straining and discarding the garlic and mint stalks. Reserve.

Next, drizzle the lamb chops with olive oil and season well before placing on the grill or barbecue. Cook for 3–4 minutes on each side or until they are nicely charred, the fat is golden and crisp and the meat is pink in the middle. The meat should spring back a little, when prodded with your finger. When done, remove the chops from the grill or barbecue and leave to rest in a warm spot for a few minutes.

Meanwhile, bring a medium-sized saucepan of salted water to a rapid boil over a high heat. Add the peas, beans and asparagus to the water and cook for 3–4 minutes, or until just tender. Drain well and transfer the vegetables to a bowl. Pour over the infused oil and season well with salt and pepper. Crush the vegetables lightly with the back of a fork and mix everything well. Lastly, add the mint leaves to the vegetables.

Divide the vegetables between serving plates. Place the lamb chops on top and serve with the mint alioli.

A single vineyard Nebbiolo from Barolo or Barberesco will work well.

BRAISED LAMB SHOULDER

WITH JERUSALEM ARTICHOKE PURÉE, SALSIFY & MOSTARDA

Lamb shoulder is a wonderful, unctuous cut but needs some love and care to get just right. We slow-braise the meat in a rich stock and then reduce the liquor to create a sticky jus. Source the mustard fruits: you will be able to find them in Italian delis or online. They are quite special and work harmoniously with the rich elements of this dish. Salsify can be found in good grocers' during the winter months, although parsnips would make a suitable alternative.

Serves 4 as a main or 6–8 as a tapa

1 small shoulder of lamb, boned, trimmed of excess fat and scored through the fat

1.5 litres (approx.) red wine to cover the lamb

2 sprigs rosemary

8 cloves garlic, crushed

2 small onions, peeled, roughly diced

2 sticks celery, roughly diced

2 small carrots, peeled, roughly diced

2 bay leaves

1.5 litres dark chicken or lamb stock (see Basics)

550g Jerusalem artichokes, peeled, evenly sliced, rubbed with lemon juice

knob of unsalted butter

550g salsify, peeled, cut into batons, rubbed with lemon juice

1 small jar good-quality mustard fruits

olive oil for cooking

sea salt and black pepper

Place the lamb in a bowl, pour in the wine and add the garlic and rosemary. Leave to marinate for at least 8 hours.

Drain the lamb and reserve the wine. Pat the meat dry. Heat a casserole pan over a medium heat and add a lug of olive oil. When hot, lower in the lamb fat-side down (this is important to prevent burning!) and seal for 3 minutes, until nicely caramelised. Turn over and repeat on the other side. Add the onion, carrot, celery, and bay and lightly colour in the lamb fat and oil. When all is nicely coloured, pour in the wine, bring to the boil and then immediately lower

to a simmer. Reduce the wine steadily until it becomes a glaze. Now, pour in the stock and, again, bring to the boil and then lower to a simmer. Skim off any scum and impurities that rise to the top to ensure the clarity of the sauce. Simmer the lamb for 2–3 hours or until the meat is meltingly tender and the liquor has reduced to a glossy, rich sauce.

Meanwhile prepare the vegetables. Cook the artichokes in boiling salted water until tender. Transfer the artichokes and a little of the water into a blender and add the butter and some seasoning. Whizz for a minute or so until you

have a smooth purée. Reserve and keep warm. Place the salsify in a pan of salted water and bring to the boil. Lower to a simmer and cook for a few minutes until the salsify is just cooked. Drain well and cool. 10 minutes before the lamb is ready, heat a sauté pan over a medium heat and add a lug of olive oil. Fry the salsify on all sides until evenly caramelised. Season well and then drain on kitchen paper.

To serve, spoon the lamb onto serving plates with some of the jus and braising vegetables. Serve the purée and fried salsify alongside and top with a spoonful of mustard fruits.

A classic red from Rioja: try a 'Reserva' wine with some age, if possible.

BARBECUED LAMB

WITH BAKED SUMMER SQUASHES, ANCHOVIES, CAPERS & BROWN BUTTER

The sweet smokiness of hot charcoal on meat is divine and lamb, in particular, benefits from being barbecued. With lamb, it's all about the fat as this is where the flavour is. For this recipe, we especially like the underused neck fillet or a leg steak with creamy, white fat layered through the side. There's nothing better than slowly rendered, crispy fat served next to sweet, pink meat. Anchovies add depth of flavour but don't overpower. But be warned. If you're going to barbecue fatty cuts, be prepared for a bit of smoke and flame!

Serves 4 as a main or
6–8 as a tapa

700g lamb neck fillet or lamb leg steaks, cut into 4 even portions

1.2kg summer squash or about 2 butternut squashes, unpeeled, cut into wedges

1 red chilli, cut in half, seeds removed, roughly chopped

2 cloves garlic, peeled, roughly chopped

100g softened unsalted butter

1 tablespoon blossom honey

30g pickled miniature capers

zest and juice of ½ lemon

4 salted anchovy fillets, finely chopped

olive oil for cooking

sea salt and black pepper

Preheat the oven to 200°C.

Put the lamb portions in a bowl, drizzle with olive oil and season with salt and pepper. Leave to marinate while the squash is cooking.

Place the squash on a baking tray. Drizzle with olive oil and spoon over the chilli, garlic, half of the butter and season well. Using your hands, mix everything together, fully coating the squash with the other ingredients. Place in the oven and cook for 10 minutes until the squash starts to caramelise, then turn the heat down to 180°C. Continue to cook for another 20 minutes until the squash becomes soft and tender. Turn the squash twice during this process to ensure even colouring and so that the squash doesn't stick. When the squash is cooked, drizzle with the honey and reserve.

Heat a grill pan or barbecue to maximum heat. Place the lamb on the grill or barbecue and cook for 3–4 minutes on either side or until nicely charred and the meat has a spring when pushed with a finger. The meat should be rosy pink inside. Rest in a warm spot. Place a saucepan over a high heat and add the remaining butter. Cook the butter until it turns nut-brown, immediately add the capers, lemon juice, zest and anchovies, season and turn off the heat. Cut the lamb into 12 slices and arrange on plates with the squash. Spoon over the butter sauce and serve.

Treat yourself with a special red from Italy. Try a super Tuscan or a red from Bolgheri.

ITALIAN-STYLE MEATBALLS
WITH SLOW-ROASTED TOMATOES & GREMOLATA

A few years back we opened the Blackfoot Butchers over the road from Salt Yard. It was an amazing experience and taught us how to use every part of the animal, wasting nothing. After butchering whole sides of cow into their various cuts, we'd inevitably have bits leftover that we would mince and turn into these delicious meatballs or 'polpette'. We sold them through the butcher's shop or transferred them to our restaurants to be cooked by the chefs. Unfortunately, the Blackfoot Butchers doesn't exist anymore – but the memory of it and this recipe do!

**Serves 4 as a main or
6–8 as a tapa**

For the meatballs:

600g good-quality beef mince

2 cloves garlic, peeled, chopped

1 tablespoon red chilli, chopped

2 tablespoon flat-leaf parsley, chopped

70g dried breadcrumbs

75ml full-cream milk

400ml dark chicken stock (see Basics)

sea salt and black pepper

For the tomatoes:

6 plum vine tomatoes

1 teaspoon thyme

1 clove garlic, peeled, finely sliced

olive oil

For the gremolata:

2 cloves garlic, peeled, chopped

zest of 2 lemons

1 tablespoon flat-leaf parsley, chopped

Preheat the oven to 130°C.

Slice the tomatoes into 3 rounds and lay them on a baking tray, sprinkle with olive oil, salt, pepper, thyme leaves and the garlic. Place in the oven and cook the tomatoes for about an hour or until they have shrunk by a third.

Mix all the ingredients for the meatballs, except the stock, in a bowl and season to taste. It's a good idea at this stage to fry a little of the meat to make sure you're happy with the seasoning. Adjust as necessary. Shape the meat into tight balls about the size of ping-pong balls. This size ensures the meatballs will be nice and juicy when cooked. Transfer the meatballs to the fridge for an hour to set.

Heat a large, deep-sided pan over a high heat and add a lug of olive oil. Add the meatballs and brown for 2 minutes on either side. Next add the chicken stock and bring to a simmer. Cook the meatballs gently for 10 minutes, turning occasionally to ensure even cooking. The stock should reduce to a sauce-like consistency but add a little more stock, if it starts to get dry.

Finally, mix together the garlic, parsley, lemon zest and a splash of olive oil to make the gremolata. Serve the meatballs on top of the tomatoes with some of the sauce and the gremolata. This dish is lovely with our olive oil mash as a side.

A Chianti Classico Riserva from Tuscany will sing well with this.

Barbecued Beef Ribeye

With Crushed Borlotti Beans & Smoked Paprika & Shallot Butter

This summer dish was created for our barbecue at Dehesa in Soho, where we have a magnificent terrace. Cooking over charcoal outdoors is one of life's fundamental pleasures. In Spain and Italy, it's also common practice to cook over wood or charcoal inside. The flavours are incredible and the sheer theatre of the barbecue gets everyone salivating before the food's even on the table. This recipe calls for ribeye as it barbecues so well due to its high marbling content. Choose a deep, red piece of meat that has been hung for at least 21 days.

**Serves 4 as a main or
6–8 as a tapa**

1kg ribeye steak or 2 x 450g steaks, left at room temperature for 20 minutes

80g unsalted butter, softened

2 large banana shallots, finely diced

1 teaspoon sweet smoked paprika

1 clove garlic, finely chopped

400g tinned borlotti beans, drained weight, washed in water

2 bunches fresh watercress

100ml extra virgin olive oil

50ml red wine vinegar, such as Cabernet Sauvignon

sea salt and black pepper

Place the butter in a bowl and add half the shallots and all the paprika. Season and mix well. Cover the shallot butter and reserve in a cool spot, but not the fridge.

Heat a medium-sized saucepan over a medium heat and add a lug of olive oil. Throw in the remaining shallots and garlic and sweat gently to cook through. Add the borlotti beans. Season well and add the extra virgin olive oil, vinegar, salt and pepper. Stir the beans and lightly crush some of them with the back of a fork. Continue cooking for 3–4 minutes, stirring as you go, and then remove from the heat and leave to cool.

Preheat the barbecue or a grill pan to maximum heat. Season the ribeye, rub with olive oil and place on the grill. Cook for 4–5 minutes on one side to achieve a good colouring. Reduce the heat to medium, turn over the ribeye and cook for a further 5–6 minutes. Press the meat with your finger: if it springs back, the meat is medium rare. When cooked to your liking, remove the steak from the heat, and transfer to a warm spot to rest. Place a few slices of the shallot butter on top so that it melts over the steak.

To serve, ladle the beans onto plates. Season and toss the watercress in olive oil and place next to the beans. Cut the steak into 4 pieces and arrange on the plates, topped with a little more of the butter.

A southern Italian red like Primitivo or Aglianico will be great with this.

Beef Sirloin With Duck Fat Chips

New Season's Garlic, Bone Marrow & Thyme Alioli

Our take on the classic steak and chips. All you need is a nicely hung, beautiful piece of beef with a good deal of marbling. Bone marrow is a great partner for beef and adds a rich, flavoursome unctuousness to the meat. Bone marrow is usually sold in the bone: to save yourself some trouble, ask your butcher to extract it for you in the shop. We sometimes fry these twice-cooked chips in Ibérico pork lard first, instead of duck fat. If you can lay your hands on it, give it a try.

**Serves 4 as a main or
6–8 as a tapa**

4 x 250g sirloin steaks, hung for at least 21 days, at room temperature

100g fresh bone marrow

2 heads new season's garlic or regular garlic

1 litre or 1kg duck fat or Ibérico pork fat, melted

4 medium King Edward or Désirée potatoes, peeled, cut into thin chips

1 litre vegetable oil

100ml homemade alioli (see Basics)

½ teaspoon fresh thyme leaves, chopped

olive oil for cooking

1 tablespoon Cabernet Sauvignon vinegar or other red wine vinegar

sea salt and black pepper

Wash the bone marrow under cold, running water for at least an hour. This process will clean the marrow and remove any bitterness. Drain well and pat dry on kitchen paper. Slice into small pieces and reserve in the fridge.

Preheat the oven to 200°C. Cut the garlic bulbs in half widthways, drizzle with olive oil and season with salt and pepper. Pop in the oven and cook for about 20 minutes or until the garlic is tender and caramelised. Reserve.

Pour the fat into a deep-sided saucepan and melt over a low heat to about 130°C or until a single chip dropped in the oil lightly bubbles but does not brown. Wash the potato chips well under cold water, drain and pat completely dry on kitchen paper. Place the chips in the fat and cook for about 7 minutes until soft and tender but without colouring. Make sure the temperature stays low. When the chips are cooked, drain well and transfer to kitchen paper.

Heat a grill pan, sauté pan or barbecue to maximum heat. Season the steaks and rub with olive oil. Cook the steaks on one side for 3–4 minutes, until nicely caramelised. Turn the meat over, lower the heat to medium, and cook for a further 4 minutes for medium steaks. The meat will give a little spring when prodded with a finger when ready. Remove the steaks from the heat and rest before serving.

To finish off the chips heat the vegetable oil in the deep-sided saucepan to 180°C or until a chip dropped in the oil browns straight away. Fry the chips until golden brown and then drain well and season with sea salt.

Finally, place the bone marrow in a small saucepan, add the vinegar and a splash of olive oil and season with salt and pepper. Warm the bone marrow until it turns translucent. Mix the thyme leaves with the alioli. To serve, spoon the bone marrow dressing onto the steaks and bring to the table with the garlic, chips and alioli on the side.

Ask for a 'Bordeaux blend' from Italy or Spain and you won't go wrong.

BRAISED OXTAIL

WITH POLENTA, CAVOLO NERO, BONE MARROW & CHILLI

Our Italian-style twist on braised beef with mash and cabbage. Oxtail has to be one of the best meats to braise. The meat is incredibly flavoursome and has that lip-sticking, unctuous quality which comes from the natural gelatin which is extracted from the bone over hours of slow cooking. Polenta is a great neutral foil for rich braises and soaks up the meat juices really well. Try to source good-quality polenta flour instead of the quick-cook variety: the results will be far superior. We've added a chilli spike to the oxtail, and finished the dish with a bone marrow vinaigrette.

Serves 4 as a main or 6–8 as a tapa

For the oxtail:

1.5kg oxtail on the bone, cut into 5cm pieces

1 litre good-quality red wine

6 cloves garlic, peeled

6 sprigs thyme

2 bay leaves

3 small carrots, peeled, roughly chopped

2 small onions, peeled, roughly chopped

3 sticks celery, chopped

1.5 litres (approx.) dark chicken stock
(see Basics)

For the polenta:

125g Bramata polenta flour, or similar quality

180ml full cream milk

180ml water

20g unsalted butter

25g grated Parmesan

sea salt and black pepper

To finish:

50g net weight beef bone marrow, cut into
2mm slices and soaked in cold water
(a butcher will be able to source this for you)

1 red chilli, deseeded, finely sliced

2 tablespoons Cabernet Sauvignon vinegar or
red wine vinegar

4 tablespoons extra virgin olive oil

200g cavolo nero leaves or curly kale,
trimmed

olive oil for cooking

Place the oxtail in a container along with the wine, garlic, thyme and bay. Put in the fridge for about 12 hours. Drain the oxtail (reserving the marinade) and pat dry on kitchen paper.

Preheat the oven to 150°C. Heat a heavy-bottomed, ovenproof casserole over a high heat and add a lug of olive oil. Add a few of the oxtail pieces and briskly colour on all sides until evenly browned. Remove the oxtail from the pan and then repeat the process with the remaining oxtail pieces. In the same pan, heat another lug of olive oil and sauté the diced vegetables until cooked and lightly caramelised. Place the oxtail pieces back in the casserole, along with the reserved marinade. Turn

the heat up to maximum and reduce the mari-nade by three quarters. Pour in the chicken stock and bring to the boil. Lower the heat and cook at a slow simmer, skimming off any scum or impurities that rise to the surface. Place a lid on the casserole and transfer to the oven. The oxtail will take about 2½ hours to cook. During this time the sauce will thicken and grow richly flavoursome, and the meat will become very tender. If you feel the sauce needs extra thickening, add a knob of butter mixed with flour towards the end of the cooking time.

To make the polenta, place a heavy-bottomed saucepan over a medium heat, pour in the milk and water and bring to the boil. Gradually whisk in the polenta until fully mixed, then lower the heat to a simmer. Cook slowly for about 30 minutes, occasionally whisking to prevent the mixture from sticking. When it is smooth and fully cooked, add the butter and Parmesan and season. Whisk again and turn off the heat.

Bring a pan of salted water to the boil and blanche the cavolo nero for 2 minutes or until tender. Drain and season. In a small saucepan, slowly warm the vinegar, extra virgin olive oil, chilli and drained bone marrow for about 3 minutes. Season.

Spoon out the polenta onto serving plates, followed by the cavolo nero, and then spoon over the oxtail and some of the rich sauce. Pour over some of the bone marrow vinaigrette and serve.

An Amarone from Italy is rich and full-bodied, just like this dish.

Pan-Roasted Rose Veal Cutlet
With Sage, Lemon, Raisins & Pine Nuts

Here we give delicious rose veal an Italian treatment using the classic combination of sage, lemon, pine nuts and raisins. Rose veal has more bite and pronounced flavour than the intensively reared varieties so can stand up to stronger sauces and garnishes without losing its identity. Cooking the meat on the bone helps keep the meat moist, adds flavour and conducts the heat ensuring an even cooking throughout. Rose veal cutlets also look very impressive on the plate. Some sautéed spinach and roasted, garlic potatoes alongside would make this a fantastic Sunday lunch alternative.

Serves 4 as a main or

6–8 as a tapa

4 rose veal cutlets (approx. 300g each with bone)

150g unsalted butter, diced

2 tablespoons raisins

2 tablespoons pine nuts

large handful sage leaves, roughly chopped

juice and zest of 1 lemon

1 tablespoon dried breadcrumbs

olive oil for cooking

sea salt and black pepper

Heat a sauté pan large enough to fit 4 cutlets in over a high heat and, when hot, add a good lug of olive oil. Season the cutlets well on both sides and place in the pan. Cook for 3–4 minutes on one side, until the veal colours and caramelises, and then turn over to cook for another 2 minutes on the other side. Now turn the heat down to medium and add the butter, raisins and pine nuts. Continue cooking on a medium heat until the butter has started to turn nut-brown and then add the sage leaves and lemon juice. Turn over the cutlets and baste with the buttery juices. Scrape the bottom of the pan to loosen any sediment and deglaze, then turn the heat down to low. You want the cutlets to cook to medium. Give them a prod with your finger: there should be a spring in the flesh when ready. When the cutlets are cooked, remove from the pan and rest for 3–4 minutes in a warm spot.

Make the sauce by adding the breadcrumbs to the lemon and butter juices in the pan and seasoning with salt and pepper. Stir the sauce well and pour in the juices that have run from the resting cutlets.

Place the cutlets on plates, spoon over the sauce and sprinkle with grated lemon zest.

A full-bodied white or light red from Sicily will match wonderfully.

GRILLED VENISON HAUNCH
WITH FARRO SALAD & GREEN PEPPERCORN DRESSING

At Dehesa, Head Chef Giancarlo Vatteroni has established himself as an exciting, creative force in the kitchen. His eclectic style reflects time spent travelling the world as well as training in game-changing restaurants such as Moro and The Sugar Club. Venison is such a delicious meat, yet is relatively underused. Being so lean, it's a great healthy choice. Venison can be found year-round, which makes it perfect for summer salads as in this recipe, as well as for the heavier, richer dishes usually associated with the meat.

Serves 4 as a main or 6–8 as a tapa

For the salad:

4 venison steaks

120g farro

4 artichokes in oil

250g cherry tomatoes

180g piquillo peppers

400g tin chickpeas, drained

small handful mint leaves

olive oil for cooking

sea salt and black pepper

For the peppercorn dressing:

3 teaspoons green peppercorns (fresh is ideal)

1 clove garlic, peeled, chopped

3 teaspoons coriander, chopped

3 teaspoons parsley, chopped

1 teaspoon lemon zest

½ teaspoon red chilli, chopped

50ml Moscatel vinegar or white balsamic vinegar

100ml extra virgin olive oil

Soak the farro overnight. If you can't find farro, replace with couscous, pearl barley or any grain you like – follow the cooking instructions on the packet.

Place the farro in a saucepan and cover with cold water. Bring to the boil and then simmer for about 20 minutes until the farro is soft and tender. Drain well and rinse under cold water for a few minutes to get rid of the starch. Put to one side.

For the dressing, use a pestle and mortar to crush the green peppercorns and garlic to a paste. Transfer the paste to a bowl and mix in the rest of the ingredients, combining well. Reserve.

Heat a grill pan or a large sauté pan to maximum heat. Rub the venison steaks with olive oil and season. Cook for 4 minutes on each side or until the outside is seared and the inside is medium rare. Let the steaks rest for 5 minutes before slicing into strips.

To assemble the salad, quarter the artichokes, halve the cherry tomatoes and cut the piquillo peppers into strips. Place in a large mixing bowl with the other salad ingredients, including the slices of venison. Season with salt and pepper and add the green peppercorn dressing. Combine everything together and then divide between serving bowls and serve.

A Tempranillo from Ribero del Duero in Spain will have the power and flavour to match fantastically.

VEGETABLES

The humble vegetable has had something of a renaissance in recent years. Once the sidekick of meat and fish, vegetables often have their own section on the menu now – or indeed in some restaurants have taken over the starring role. This championing of the vegetable is long overdue and something we've always advocated. We pride ourselves on our vegetable-based tapas. Whether it's dark green cavolo nero from Northern Italy in December, exquisite asparagus from the Wye Valley in June, or ripe, plump tomatoes from Andalusia in September, we find the best seasonal produce and put it to good use in our kitchens. We're all for sourcing as close to home as possible, but we simply don't have the baking sun of the Mediterranean to intensify the flavours and natural juices of such fruits and vegetables as tomatoes, peppers, citrus fruits, apricots and figs. Consequently, we're quite happy to sit fresh English peas next to Spanish broad beans and shave over a summer truffle from Italy – and enjoy the best of three worlds.

Wild mushrooms and fungi are a favourite at the restaurants, and a highlight of the year is the porcini, or cep, season. These mushrooms, generally sourced from Umbria, are so meaty and flavoursome that they could almost be a protein. We like to roast them simply in some olive oil and butter and finish with a little sliced garlic. Girolles, grown in Italy and parts of the UK, appear in the spring and are at their most delicious cooked quickly and simply, with perhaps a fried free-range egg, a scattering of pine nuts and a splash of sherry.

Britain has an amazing selection of root vegetables and in the winter months we make use of the glut. Parsnips, swedes and turnips are excellent when oven-roasted until they caramelise, or cooked slowly in milk and blended to make a rich, comforting purée. We love using Britain's wonderful potato crop to make patatas fritas and bravas or to whip into a silky olive oil mash.

Green-leaved vegetables such as British large leaf spinach and Italian cavolo nero and turnip tops are great briefly cooked in boiling water, then immediately cooled and dressed simply in olive oil and lemon to showcase their unique flavours.

Our signature dish is deep-fried courgette flowers stuffed with goat's cheese. They are so popular that we buy the flowers year-round so not to upset our regulars. They're available from the UK, Spain and Italy in the summer, and out of season we buy them from Israel, Holland and France.

As with all produce, buy the best you can and try to use vegetables and fruit which are in season, as they will be tastier, more vibrant and probably more economical. When approaching the recipes that follow, try to think of vegetables in a different way: make them the star of the show and give them all the love, care and attention you might normally bestow on meat or fish.

Gratin Of Jerusalem Artichoke
Cavolo Nero, Kale & Smoked Garlic

Our gratins are very popular over the winter months. Rich and delicious, they arrive at the table with a golden crust and creamy sauce bubbling away around the sides like a volcano about to erupt. Here we combine the unique, earthy flavour of Jerusalem artichokes with a mixture of winter greens: kale and cavolo nero. Smoked garlic is an unusual addition, but regular garlic will also suffice.

**Serves 4 as a main or
6–8 as a tapa or starter**

800ml double cream

4 cloves smoked or regular garlic, peeled, finely sliced

200g pecorino or other semi-hard, salty Italian cheese, grated

1kg Jerusalem artichokes, peeled, sliced into even rounds

120g cavolo nero or savoy cabbage

120g curly kale

1 handful fresh or dried bread-crumbs with an irregular texture

extra virgin olive oil

sea salt and black pepper

Preheat the grill to 160°C.

Pour the double cream into a small saucepan and set over a medium heat. Add the sliced garlic to the cream. Reduce slowly by half. Stir in the grated cheese and reserve.

Bring a pan of salted water to the boil, turn down to a simmer and add the artichokes. Cook for 3–4 minutes until just tender. Drain well and reserve. Bring another pan of salted water to the boil and blanche the greens for 2 minutes. Drain well, ensuring there is no excess liquid in the greens as this will dilute the cream. Reserve.

Season the artichokes with salt and pepper and spread over the base of 4 terracotta heat-proof dishes (approx. 13cm in diameter) or one large one. Spread the greens on top and then pour over the cream, distributing it evenly. Scatter with the breadcrumbs, drizzle with a lug of extra virgin olive oil and place under the grill. Grill until the cream is hot and the breadcrumbs are golden brown. Bring, bubbling hot, to the table and serve.

A full-bodied white from Southern Italy will stand up to the strong flavours of this dish.

Courgette Flowers

Stuffed With Goat's Cheese & Drizzled With Honey

These courgette flowers helped put Salt Yard on the map when we first opened. The genius behind them lies in their simplicity and the perfect combination of sweet and salty flavours and crisp and runny textures. We sell about 100,000 of these a year across the restaurants and literally can't take them off the menu! Courgette flowers are in season in the UK from early summer to September and there are plenty around, making them ideal for a summer dinner party. It's important you choose a semi-firm goat's cheese so that it only partially melts when deep-fried.

Makes 12 courgette flowers

12 courgette flowers, stalks intact

120g semi-firm goat's cheese, such as Monte Enebro or Chèvre, cut into 10g pieces

runny blossom honey for drizzling

2 litres vegetable oil for frying

For the batter:

150g plain flour, sifted

2 teaspoons baking powder

450ml sparkling water

To make the batter, place the flour and baking powder in a bowl and whisk in the water, ensuring everything mixes well. Cover and leave to rest for half an hour.

Carefully peel back the delicate petals of each flower and remove the stamens as they can taste bitter. Shape the goat's cheese into balls and gently stuff into each flower. Twist the petals to form a tight seal around the cheese, taking care not to tear them. Cut a small slit in the bottom of each courgette stalk to help speed up the cooking process.

Pour the vegetable oil into a deep-sided pan. Heat the oil until a drop of batter fizzles and browns as soon as it is dribbled into the oil or to 180°C if using a deep-fat fryer. Dip the flowers into the batter and then lower into the frying pan. It's best to deep-fry in batches of two or three at a time. Cook the flowers, turning occasionally, until they are golden brown on all sides. This should take 3–5 minutes. When ready, remove the flowers from the oil, drain well on kitchen paper and keep warm. Cook the remaining flowers in the same manner. When all the flowers have been cooked and drained of oil, transfer to serving plates. Drizzle with runny blossom honey. Serve straight away.

A left-field and delicious match with this is a medium-sweet Oloroso.

Ricotta Gnocchi
With Spring Vegetables & Pesto

The credit for this beautiful dish goes to Jamie Thickett, our talented Head Chef at Opera Tavern. It's typical of Jamie's light, vibrant style of cooking. The gnocchi are easy to make and can be served as the carbohydrate alongside many other dishes like grilled fish or meat, or simply tossed in a tomato sauce. The spring vegetables can be varied according to taste and what's available at the market. Green vegetables, such as peas, green beans or young spinach leaves, work particularly well. The wild garlic leaf may be replaced by a garlic clove.

Serves 4 as a main or

6–8 as a tapa

For the gnocchi:

250g ricotta

2 egg yolks

20g Parmesan, grated

110g Tipo '00' pasta flour

extra flour for dusting

sea salt and black pepper

For the pesto:

1 large bunch basil, stalk included

50g pine nuts, lightly toasted

25g Parmesan

30g wild garlic or 1 clove garlic, peeled

150ml extra virgin olive oil

For the vegetables:

300g purple sprouting broccoli or tenderstem, trimmed

16 spears asparagus, trimmed

100g baby Swiss chard or young spinach, trimmed

50g broad beans, fresh or frozen

To make the pesto, put the basil, pine nuts, Parmesan and wild garlic (or garlic clove) in a blender. Put the lid on and, gradually adding the olive oil, blend to a purée. Season well.

To make the gnocchi, strain the ricotta for a few minutes in a sieve or through a cloth to remove any excess liquid. Place the ricotta in a bowl and mix in the eggs and Parmesan. Then gradually add the flour, mixing as you go, and season. Place the gnocchi dough on top of a floured work surface. Divide into 4 pieces and roll each piece into a long sausage with the diameter of a 2-pound coin. Cut each length into bite-sized pieces and place on a chopping board or tray so they can easily be tipped into a pan. Bring a large pan of salted water to the boil and then slide the gnocchi into the bubbling water. They're cooked when they rise to the surface. Remove from the water with a slotted spoon and place in a dish. Season and keep warm.

Cook the vegetables in a large pan of boiling salted water. Firstly, cook the broccoli for 3 minutes or so until al dente, remove from the pan with a slotted spoon and keep warm. Next add the beans, chard or spinach along with the asparagus and cook for a further 2–3 minutes, or until the vegetables are all just cooked through. Drain well in a colander and press lightly to release any excess moisture. Season well and toss together with the reserved broccoli. Ladle out the gnocchi onto serving dishes, top with the vegetables and spoon over the pesto. Serve.

Garnacha Blanca from Spain is a great white variety that will pair harmoniously.

FRESH PASTA

Fresh pasta is one of life's joys and once you've mastered the rolling process, you may never look back. We use a pasta machine at work and it's worth buying a small one to have at home. They're widely available, inexpensive and produce perfect pasta: silky thin and all of an even thickness. Use this base to make tagliatelle, pappardelle and ravioli. Try to use organic eggs as their yolks tend to be really yellow, making the pasta an attractive golden colour.

500g Tipo '00' pasta flour

16 medium free-range or organic egg yolks

sea salt and black pepper

Place the pasta flour in a bowl and make a well in the centre. Season and then gradually add the yolks whilst mixing with the tips of your fingers. Continue mixing until all the yolks are incorporated into the flour. Now, with both hands, knead the dough back and forth in the bowl until it has come together and is elastic and smooth.

If the mix feels particularly wet or sticky, knead in some extra Tipo '00' flour and continue kneading until the pasta is firm to the touch but not dry or overly hard. If the dough doesn't bind, add more egg yolks. Wrap in cling film and rest in the fridge for 1 hour before using.

To prepare your dough for cutting into tagliatelle, pappardelle or ravioli, put it through the pasta machine. Divide the dough into 4, wrapping 3 of the pieces in cling film to prevent them from drying out whilst you work. Roll out the other piece of dough on a floured surface until it's about 1cm thick and narrow enough to fit through the slot of the pasta machine. Run the pasta through the pasta machine on each setting, folding it in half between each roll. Keep rolling until the penultimate setting, and then repeat the whole process starting at the thickest setting, and again finishing on the second-to-last setting. This double-rolling process will strengthen the pasta and make the finished result smoother. You should now have a silky, elastic pasta sheet that you can cut. If the pasta seems to be getting a little soft or damp, then add a dusting of extra flour as you go. The pasta is now ready to be cut.

Fresh Pasta

With Lemon, Marjoram & Parmesan

This is a very simple recipe based on the lovely, fresh flavours of marjoram and lemon which conjure up Southern Italy. Use the fresh pasta recipe to make some lovely wide pappardelle strips. Of course, you could use good-quality, fresh, shop-bought pasta to save on time, but we urge you to try making your own!

**Serves 4 as a main or
6–8 as a tapa**

500g homemade pasta sheets (see page 130) or good-quality, shop-bought egg pasta such as pappardelle

Tipo '00' pasta flour for dusting

juice of 2 lemons

2 lemons, peeled, segmented and segments diced

120g unsalted butter, diced

500g Parmesan, grated

4 tablespoons marjoram or oregano leaves

extra virgin olive oil for finishing

sea salt and black pepper

To make the fresh pasta use a machine to roll out the dough to the penultimate thickness (see page 130). When the pasta is rolled, cut it lengthwise into 3cm-wide strips to make pappardelle. Dust again with flour and hang over a long wooden pole to dry out.

Now heat the lemon juice in a medium-sized saucepan over a high heat. Reduce the lemon juice to a light glaze and set aside.

To cook the pasta, set a large pan of water on a high heat and bring to the boil with plenty of sea salt. Carefully slide the pasta from the pole into the boiling water and give it a swirl with a wooden spoon. Cook until al dente, which will just take a few minutes. When ready, reserve a cup of the cooking liquor and then drain the rest of the pasta in a colander. Pour the pasta water into the pan with the lemon juice and turn the heat back to maximum. When the water is boiling, whisk in the diced butter and Parmesan until they have blended together. Now, work-ing quickly, transfer the drained pasta into the thickened water and lemon juice and stir rapidly with some tongs or a wooden spoon. This action will help the sauce thicken further and ensure the pasta is fully coated. Finally add the marjoram leaves, lemon segments and a good grind of black pepper. Toss the pasta in the sauce once more, divide between serving bowls and drizzle over some extra virgin olive oil. Serve the pasta piping hot.

Arneis from Piedmont in Italy has the zest and aroma to work well here.

BLACK OLIVE RAVIOLI

WITH PARSLEY SAUCE

We love making fresh pasta at the restaurants. Ravioli, in particular, are versatile and great for making in advance. The beauty of homemade pasta is that you only need the simplest of fillings to make a superb lunch or mid-week supper. Good-quality olives are paramount here as they're the predominant ingredient and flavour in this recipe. We use delicious Spanish Aragón olives, which are quite sweet and almost nutty.

Serves 4 as a main or

6–8 as a tapa or starter

500g homemade pasta sheets
(see page 130)

Tipo '00' pasta flour for dusting

egg yolk for egg wash

For the filling:

120g black olives, pitted, such as

Aragón or Kalamata

2 cloves garlic, finely chopped

1 tablespoon capers

zest and juice of 1 lemon

20g anchovy fillets (optional)

2 tablespoons extra virgin olive oil

sea salt and black pepper

For the parsley sauce:

1 litre dark chicken stock or

vegetable stock (see Basics)

500ml double cream

1 large bunch flat-leaf parsley

extra virgin olive oil for finishing

Parmesan or Pecorino for finishing

Place all the ingredients for the filling in a blender or food processor and pulse until you have a fairly smooth paste. Reserve in the fridge.

To make the sauce place the stock in a saucepan and reduce over a high heat until thick and syrupy. Add the cream and reduce by half. Add the chopped parsley and cook for 2–3 minutes. Transfer the mix into a blender and pulse until you have a smooth sauce. Reserve, keeping warm.

To form the ravioli roll out 4 sheets of pasta to the penultimate thickness (see page 130). Lay 1 of the pasta sheets on a floured work surface and place teaspoonfuls of the olive filling on the sheet at 3cm intervals. Brush the pasta sheet with egg wash and carefully lay another sheet of pasta on top. Press the pasta down around the edges of the mounds of filling to seal and form ravioli shapes. Cut out the ravioli – either into circles, using a pastry cutter, or into squares, using a sharp knife. Repeat the process with the other 2 sheets of pasta.

Set a large pan of salted water over a medium heat and bring to the boil. Transfer the ravioli onto a large plate and then slide into the boiling water. Cook for about 3 minutes, until the pasta is just cooked and the filling hot. Divide the ravioli between serving plates and spoon over the parsley sauce. Serve with a drizzle of extra virgin olive oil and some grated hard cheese, if you like.

A light Barbera d'Asti from Piedmont is a red that makes for a surprisingly good match.

Truffled Macaroni

Andrew Clarke, our brilliant Head Chef at Salt Yard, has created something of a signature dish with his spin on macaroni cheese. We probably all remember this comfort food favourite from childhood days, with its rich, cheese-laden sauce, stodgy, overcooked pasta and crisp, cheesy topping. Andrew has taken the Salt Yard version to new, more refined heights. Three different types of Italian cheese add great depth of flavour and complexity to the dish and the truffle lends a sublime luxuriousness. We've added some fried breadcrumbs, or migas, for textural contrast.

Serves 4 as a main or
6–8 as a tapa

250g good-quality dried tubetti or short macaroni pasta

500ml milk

400ml double cream

90g Fontina or Taleggio, grated

90g Parmesan, grated

100g buffalo mozzarella, cut into small chunks

2 teaspoons Dijon mustard

1 tablespoon white truffle oil

100g dried breadcrumbs

1 small black truffle, grated (optional)

olive oil for cooking

sea salt and black pepper

Preheat the oven to 180°C.

In a large, wide-based saucepan, bring the milk and cream to a boil, then bring down to a simmer. Add the 3 cheeses and stir with a wooden spoon until the cheese has melted. Turn up the heat to medium and add the pasta. Continue stirring, until the pasta is just cooked, or al dente. When you stir the pasta, be sure to scrape the bottom of the pan to ensure nothing sticks. As soon as the pasta is cooked, add the mustard, truffle oil and season with salt and pepper to taste. If you are a truffle fan, then add some more truffle oil!

While cooking the pasta, make the breadcrumbs. Heat a small sauté pan over a medium heat and add 2 good lugs of olive oil. When the oil is hot, add the breadcrumbs and season with salt and pepper. Fry the breadcrumbs, stirring as you go, until they are golden brown and crisp. Remove the pan from the heat and tip the breadcrumbs onto kitchen paper to drain.

Spoon the pasta into a medium-sized serving dish and sprinkle with the fried breadcrumbs. Place in the oven for 10 minutes to lightly brown. At the table, grate the truffle, if desired, over the macaroni.

There's nothing wrong with oaky Chardonnay; one from Tuscany will be lovely with this.

Cauliflower & Truffle Risotto
With Egg Yolk

Cauliflower and truffle? An unlikely partnership, you may think, but they are a match made in heaven. The luxurious kick of the truffle works perfectly with the earthy sweetness of cooked cauliflower. This is a poor man's risotto given a glamorous edge! You'll need to use good stock here – either chicken or vegetable – and do try to track down some fresh, black truffle. If you can't find truffle, don't worry, truffle oil will do. Egg yolk, stirred into the rice just before serving adds a deep, rich finish and pulls together the whole dish.

Serves 4 as a main or
6–8 as a starter or tapa

320g Arborio or Carnaroli risotto rice

1 litre (approx.) chicken or vegetable stock (see Basics)

½ head cauliflower, broken down into florets

3 banana shallots, finely chopped

1 large glass of white wine

100g unsalted butter, diced

20g Parmesan, grated

olive oil for cooking

3 tablespoons truffle oil

4–6 free-range egg yolks, depending on the number of plates

1 small black truffle (optional)

sea salt and black pepper

Slice the cauliflower florets finely, trying to retain their natural shape. Heat a sauté pan over a medium heat and add a lug of olive oil. When the pan is hot, add the cauliflower and season. Lower the heat and cook the florets until lightly coloured and just tender. Set aside.

Place the stock in a saucepan and bring to a simmer. Heat a saucepan over a medium heat, add a lug of olive oil and the shallots. Cook until soft but without colour. Next add the rice and stir well, coating it in the oil and shallots. After a minute, pour in the wine, bring to the boil and reduce the wine. Stir the rice continuously so it doesn't catch. When the rice has absorbed most of the wine, start ladling in the hot stock gradually, waiting for it to be absorbed by the rice before adding more. It will take about 15–17 minutes for the rice to be cooked al dente and the stock to be absorbed. The rice should be thick and creamy enough for a spoon to leave a faint trail in it.

Turn the heat down to very low and add the Parmesan, cauliflower slices and the butter. Stir well and continue to cook for another minute. The rice should be rich and creamy. Add the truffle oil and season well.

Turn off the heat and allow the risotto to sit for a minute before spooning into serving bowls. Top each bowl with an egg yolk and season. Slice over the truffle, if using. Encourage your guests to stir in the yolk before eating.

Try a full-bodied, white blend from Priorat, Spain.

Peas, Broad Beans & Asparagus
With Summer Truffle Butter & Pea Shoot Salad

This recipe couldn't be simpler and really is the essence of spring on a plate. Throughout the spring months, peas and beans are available from Spain, Italy and the UK, and are all equally delicious. The summer truffle butter adds a luxurious flavour to the dish and combines with the juices of the sweet vegetables to create a lovely sauce which brings the whole dish together. This would be ideal as part of a spring lunch or as an accompaniment to the barbecued lamb with baked summer squashes.

Serves 4 as a main or

6–8 as a starter or tapa

50g butter at room temperature

½ teaspoon white truffle oil

1 small truffle, grated (optional)

50g broad beans, shelled
(fresh or frozen)

200g fresh peas

16 spears asparagus, trimmed,
cut in half widthwise

50g pea shoots

2 tablespoons classic vinaigrette
(see Basics)

a few slices of truffle for the salad
(optional)

sea salt and black pepper

Place the softened butter in a bowl and add the truffle oil and grated truffle, if you're using this. Season with salt and pepper. Knead the butter to incorporate the flavourings. Wrap the butter in a large piece of cling film, shaping it into a cylinder as you do so. Transfer the butter to the fridge and chill for at least 1 hour.

Heat a medium-sized saucepan over a medium heat and add about 300ml water. Bring the water to the boil and add the vegetables. Season with salt and pepper and cook for 2 minutes or until the water has nearly evaporated. Now take the truffle butter, cut into dice and add to the vegetables in the pan. Turn the heat down to low and let the butter melt, combining with the vegetable juices.

In a small bowl, mix the pea shoots with the vinaigrette, seasoning and truffle slices, if you're using.

Divide the vegetables between serving plates, spoon over the buttery juices and top with the dressed pea shoots.

A Sauvignon Blanc from Alto Adige in Northeast Italy.

Grilled Asparagus

With Quail's Eggs, Sherry Vinegar & Goat's Curd

English asparagus has a very short season, usually from the beginning of April to the end of June. When it arrives, it sends the food world into a frenzy. It's difficult to pinpoint the flavour of this vegetable but we'd describe it as the flavour of spring in a stem! Asparagus and eggs are a classic partnership and here we use quail's eggs – soft-boiled so the yolk mollifies the sweet sharpness of the vinegar and the smoky juices of the grilled asparagus. A fresh, creamy goat's curd or soft goat's cheese finishes the dish.

Serves 4 as a starter or as a light main

20 thick spears asparagus
(5 spears or about 120g per portion)

16 quail's eggs

150g goat's curd or soft, fresh goat's cheese

2 tablespoons sherry vinegar

2 tablespoons extra virgin olive oil

olive oil for cooking

sea salt and black pepper

Take your asparagus spears and trim the very ends with a knife. If the stems are fresh and crisp, you won't need to do anything further. If they're woody or dry, trim the stalks a little further up and gently peel the stems. This will rid the asparagus of its tough, inedible, outer skin. Place the asparagus in a bowl, drizzle with olive oil, season with salt and pepper and toss all together.

Cook the quail's eggs in boiling salted water for 2½ minutes. Drain the eggs and run them under cold water to arrest the cooking process. This should take about 2 minutes or so. When the eggs are cooled, crack them carefully all over and peel them under cold running water. The eggs are soft so you must treat them gently.

Preheat a grill pan or barbecue to a high heat. Lay the asparagus on the grill and cook for about 3 minutes on each side or until the spears are lightly charred, caramelised and tender. Transfer the spears to a bowl, sprinkle with the sherry vinegar and the extra virgin olive oil and toss.

You can now divide the asparagus between your serving plates and scatter with the goat's cheese, broken into bite-sized, rustic chunks. Slice the quail's eggs through the middle and lay them on top of the asparagus.

Kerner, a white variety from Northeast Italy, will pair beautifully.

Salad Of Trevise

Roasted Pears, Fresh Chestnuts & Marjoram

This seasonal salad is inspired by the flavours of Italy. Trevise is a wonderful fleshy lettuce with a unique bitter-sweet flavour that is only available during the winter months – although you could substitute radicchio which is readily available year-round. The salad uses sweet, caramelised pears and an unusual dressing made from chestnut honey. We finish the dish with shaved fresh chestnuts for a nutty edge and pungent marjoram for its heady aroma and flavour. The addition of salty gorgonzola and croutons would make this into a substantial lunch.

Serves 4 as a starter or tapa

1 large head trevise, stem removed, leaves cut roughly

1 small Packham pear, peeled, quartered, core removed

1 large pinch caster sugar for caramelising the pears

1 handful wild rocket leaves, trimmed, washed

1 chestnut, fresh or tinned, shelled, sliced very finely

1 teaspoon marjoram leaves

For the dressing:

1 tablespoon chestnut honey

1 small teaspoon Dijon mustard

1 tablespoon Moscatel vinegar

2½ tablespoons extra virgin olive oil

a squeeze of lemon juice

sea salt and black pepper

Heat a non-stick pan over a medium heat. Add the pears and a sprinkling of caster sugar. Toss the pears to coat with the sugar, and cook, moving the pears about the pan, until the sugar starts to caramelise. Turn down the heat and cook until the pears have softened and are nicely golden brown. Remove the pears from the pan and cool. Once cooled, slice each quarter into four.

Whisk together the honey and mustard in a bowl, and then whisk in the vinegar followed by the olive oil. Season with salt and pepper and a squeeze of lemon juice. If the dressing looks too thick, add a splash of warm water.

Place the trevise and rocket in a mixing bowl and season well. Toss the leaves together and add the marjoram, sliced chestnut and pear and then the vinaigrette. Toss together again and check the seasoning, before dividing the salad between serving plates.

A Friulano white wine from Northeast Italy will be a perfect pairing.

Baked Baby Peppers

Stuffed With Summer Vegetables & Basil

Vibrant flavours and colours make this dish sing of the Mediterranean in summer. Baby peppers are perfect for tapas: lightly roasted and then loaded with roasted vegetables, chilli and basil, they always look impressive and are easy to pick up and eat with your fingers. A good grocer will be able to source them for you, but feel free to use regular red peppers if you want a more substantial dish. We stuff our peppers with aubergine, courgette, fennel and cherry tomatoes, though sundried tomatoes, olives or even goat's cheese would work just as well.

Serves 4 as a meal or

6–8 as canapés or tapas

16 red baby peppers or

4 medium-sized red peppers

1 small head fennel, core removed, finely diced

2 cloves garlic, peeled, finely chopped

1 aubergine, finely diced

1 chilli, deseeded, finely chopped

1 large courgette, finely diced

12 cherry tomatoes, cut into quarters

1 small handful basil leaves

olive oil for cooking

sea salt and black pepper

Preheat the oven to 220°C.

Place the peppers on a baking tray, sprinkle with olive oil and salt, and place in the oven for about 25 minutes or until the peppers are softened and the skins lightly blistered. You may need to turn the peppers once or twice to ensure even cooking. Check that the tops of the peppers are cooked too. Remove from the oven and allow to cool down.

Turn the oven down to 190°C. Heat a large sauté pan over a medium heat and add a lug of olive oil. When the pan is hot, add the fennel and garlic. Cook briskly without colouring for 2 minutes and then add the aubergine and chilli. Cook for a further 2 minutes and then add the courgette and tomato. Stir everything and season well. Continue cooking until all the vegetables have cooked through and begun to caramelise. The tomatoes should break down along with the vegetables, creating a thick sauce. When done, tear over some of the basil leaves and stir through.

To stuff the peppers, slice off the tops and retain. Nick the very bottom off the peppers so there is a flat surface for them to rest on once stuffed. Remove and discard the seeds. Stuff the roasted vegetable mix into the peppers, pressing it inside gently with a spoon. Place the lids back on the peppers and transfer to the oven again to heat through. Serve with more roughly-torn basil leaves scattered on top and extra virgin olive oil drizzled over.

Try to find Belondrade y Lurton, one of Spain's finest white wines or try a Riesling from Northern Italy.

Crispy Duck Egg Yolk

With Celeriac Purée & Seasonal Wild Mushrooms

This is a wonderful starter or tapa for the winter months. Earthy, meaty wild mushrooms are paired with a rich, velvety celeriac purée and then finished with a deep-fried duck egg yolk. It's a hearty dish that will pacify even the staunchest of meat lovers! Celeriac is a big favourite with us. It's almost as versatile as the potato, and can be roasted, mashed, puréed or deep-fried. Don't be put off by its ugly appearance; its rough exterior hides some very tasty flesh indeed. Try to use free-range or organic duck's eggs here, if possible.

Serves 4 as a starter or
6–8 as tapas

1 medium celeriac, peeled, diced

400–500ml full cream milk

4 duck's eggs

plain flour for dredging

panko-style breadcrumbs for coating

1 large egg, beaten

250g mixed wild or cultivated mushrooms, trimmed, washed in cold water (Meaty, textured mushrooms are better as they hold their weight. Mushrooms shrink significantly when cooked, hence the large quantity needed)

1 tablespoon flat-leaf parsley, finely chopped

1 garlic clove, finely chopped

a squeeze of lemon juice

olive oil for cooking

extra virgin olive oil for finishing

sea salt and black pepper

To make the celeriac purée, place the diced celeriac in a medium-sized saucepan, add the milk and season with salt and pepper. Bring to the boil and then lower to a simmer. Cook for about 20 minutes, until very tender. Drain the celeriac, keeping the milk, and place the flesh in a blender with half the milk. Blend to a thick purée, adding more milk if it seems too thick or will not blend properly. Set aside.

Now for the yolks. Bring a small saucepan of water to the boil and then reduce to a low simmer. Have ready a container of cold water with some ice cubes in to refresh the yolks. Separate the yolks and carefully drop into the simmering water. Using a timer, cook for 2 minutes, until just set. Now quickly transfer the yolks to the iced water to cool down. Place the flour, beaten egg and breadcrumbs in 3 separate bowls ready for coating. Carefully drain the yolks. Gently roll the yolks in first the flour, then the egg, and lastly the breadcrumbs, so they're evenly coated. Set aside for a moment.

To cook the mushrooms, heat a large non-stick sauté pan over a medium heat and add a lug of olive oil. When the oil is hot, add the mushrooms and season well. Cook for 4–5 minutes, occasionally shaking the pan so that they colour evenly. Add the chopped parsley, garlic and a squeeze of lemon juice, cook a little longer and remove from the heat.

A few minutes before serving, heat a small non-stick sauté pan over a medium heat and add enough olive oil to shallow fry. When the oil is hot, add the breaded yolks and

cook until golden brown and crispy on all sides. The yolks will be runny in the middle. Remove from the oil, drain on clean kitchen paper and season with sea salt. Spoon some of the warm celeriac purée onto serving plates and then top with the mushrooms and the crisp yolk. Any juices left in the mushroom pan can be spooned over the top with a drizzling of extra virgin olive oil.

A medium-full bodied white from Friuli, North Italy.

FARRO WITH CAVOLO NERO & CHESTNUTS

A popular winter dish that would be a great accompaniment to a roast bird or some grilled oily fish like mackerel or sardines. Cooked chestnuts are widely available in supermarkets now and add a delicious, sweet nuttiness to dishes. They're also very festive so this could be an unusual addition to your Christmas lunch. Farro has a lovely texture when boiled and is a good vehicle for other ingredients and flavours. It's also a very healthy product and apparently does wonders for the digestive system. However, you could replace the farro with nutty, green lentils.

Serves 4 as a tapa or side

300g farro or green lentils, washed under running cold water

200g cavolo nero or savoy cabbage, ribs removed, cut into strips

125g cooked chestnuts, roughly crumbled

2 tablespoons extra virgin olive oil

2 tablespoons sherry vinegar

sea salt and black pepper

Place the washed farro in a saucepan and cover with cold, salted water. Bring to the boil over a high heat and then simmer for about 20 minutes until the farro is soft and tender. Drain in a colander and transfer to a mixing bowl.

Bring a separate pan of salted water to the boil and throw in the cabbage. Cook for 4 minutes or until the cabbage is cooked but with a little bite. Drain in a colander and press gently to release any excess moisture. Place the cabbage in the bowl with the farro and add the crumbled chestnuts, olive oil and vinegar. Season well with salt and pepper and mix. Finally, divide between serving dishes and finish with another sprinkling of sea salt, if you like.

For a great match, track down an oxidised-style white from Rioja in Spain.

Salad Of Italian Vegetables

With Lemon, Chilli & Garlic

In the Lazio region of Italy, seasonal vegetables are often served cold, dressed simply with a squeeze of lemon juice – or a drop of vinegar – and some good olive oil. It's a great way of showcasing the vegetables' natural flavours. For this salad, select whatever looks best from baby Swiss chard, spinach, cavolo nero, green beans, turnip tops or chicory. It's important to cook and cool down the vegetables correctly so that they retain their vibrant colours. As you're eating the vegetables cold, they want to be cooked through and not al dente.

Serves 4 as a starter, tapa or side

Choose 3 from this selection:

100g green beans, trimmed

160g cavolo nero

4 heads baby Swiss chard

160g turnip tops

160g wild chicory leaves

160g young leaf spinach

For the dressing:

1 red chilli, end trimmed, sliced through finely

2 cloves garlic, peeled, finely chopped

3 tablespoons (approx.) extra virgin olive oil

juice of ½ lemon

sea salt and black pepper

Set a large pan of salted water over a high heat and bring to the boil. You will need a large bowl of water with ice cubes waiting, so you can refresh the vegetables as soon as they are cooked.

Cook your chosen vegetables in turn in the same water. Start with the beans (if you're using beans) and cook for 4 minutes. After 4 minutes or when just cooked, remove from the pan and plunge into the iced water. Repeat this process for the other vegetables, cooking the cavolo nero and chard for 3 minutes and the turnip tops, chicory and spinach for 2 minutes. In each case, check that the vegetable is cooked and then plunge into the iced water. When the vegetables are cold, drain in a colander and press well to squeeze out any excess water.

When the vegetables are dry, transfer to a bowl and add the olive oil, chilli, garlic and lemon juice. Season with sea salt and black pepper and mix well to ensure all the vegetables are coated with the oil and lemon juice. Divide between plates and serve.

Hard-to-find, but delicious with this, would be a light white from Cinque Terre, Italy.

Parsnip Chips

With Truffle Honey & Rosemary

The sweet, earthy flavours of the parsnip are way beyond its humble origins. You can make some seriously luxurious, delicious dishes with this most common of Britain's root vegetables. Parsnip soup, for example, requires nothing more than roasted parsnips, good stock and seasoning and you have a dish that more than equals the sum of its parts. This tapa is great as part of a larger tapas meal or as an interesting vegetable side for a roast Sunday lunch. The truffle honey is simple to make: just follow the instructions in the Basics chapter.

Serves 4 as a side or

6–8 as a tapa

1.2 kg parsnips, peeled, cut into
pencil-thin strips

2 litres full cream milk

2 sprigs rosemary leaves,
finely chopped

3–4 tablespoons truffle honey
(see Basics)

1 small fresh black truffle
(optional)

olive oil for cooking

sea salt and black pepper

Preheat the oven to 210°C.

Quickly rinse the parsnip strips in cold water and then place in a large saucepan. Cover with milk, season with salt and set over a high heat. Bring the milk to the boil and then reduce to a simmer, slowly cooking the parsnips until tender. Drain the milk very well from the parsnips and discard. Lay the parsnips out on a dish to cool down for a few minutes.

You will need a deep-sided baking tray large enough to fit the parsnips. Place the roasting tray over a medium heat and pour in olive oil to about a depth of 0.5cm. Carefully place the parsnips in the oil and turn them to ensure they're fully coated. Season well and place the tray in the oven for about 20–25 minutes or until the parsnips are golden brown and crispy but not blackened. Turn the parsnips a couple of times during the cooking process to make sure they brown evenly and don't stick.

When done, transfer the parsnips to a bowl and season with salt, pepper and the chopped rosemary. Toss together – the parsnips should rustle like French fries – and then drizzle with the honey, as much, or as little, as you like. Divide the chips between bowls and grate over some fresh black truffle, if you're using, and serve piping hot.

If served as a pre-dinner nibble, go for a curve ball: red Lambrusco.

BAKED OLIVE OIL POTATOES

WITH SMOKED WILD MUSHROOMS & EGG YOLK

This is an unusual, interesting vegetarian option which you can vary according to the time of year. In the spring and summer, you can use morels or girolles and in the winter, porcini. Smoking chips are a great store cupboard item and are available at larger supermarkets and online. We like to use apple wood or hickory. Once you get through your first couple of smoking sessions, it will be like second nature. The smoking chips impart a mouthwatering, sweet-and-smoky flavour to the mushrooms, which is nicely offset by the richness of the potatoes and the egg yolk.

Serves 4 as a main or

6–8 as a starter or tapa

8 tablespoons hickory or apple wood smoking chips or

1 smoking bag

800g Jersey Royals or new potatoes, washed, dried

2 cloves garlic, peeled

1 sprig thyme

150ml extra virgin olive oil

4 tablespoons double cream

200g morels, girolles, porcini or any meaty wild mushroom, trimmed, washed

6–8 free-range eggs (Burford Browns are good), separated, yolks reserved

4 teaspoons flat-leaf parsley, chopped

sea salt and black pepper

Preheat the oven to 200°C. Cook the potatoes in boiling salted water until just tender, drain and let cool. Place the potatoes, garlic and thyme on a baking tray, drizzle with olive oil and season. Bake for 10 minutes until the skins start to blister. Remove from the oven, cool down and peel off the skins. Strain the oil and keep. Transfer the potatoes to a bowl, crush well with a fork, add the cream, the olive oil from the oven tray, season and mix well. Divide the potatoes between 4 small ovenproof serving dishes.

If you're using a smoking bag, follow the instructions on the packet. Otherwise, set up your own smoking system by putting the chips on the bottom of a small saucepan together with 2 small metal pastry cutters or rings to act as trivets. Fold a piece of aluminium foil several times to make a sturdy base that will fit the inside of the pan. Rest this on top of the trivets. Now place the pan on a high heat until the chips start to smoke. Put the mushrooms on the foil and cover the top of the pan with another layer of foil to create a smoke-tight seal. Remove the pan from the heat and let the mushrooms smoke for 6–7 minutes under the foil. They'll look soft and cooked when done.

Spoon the mushrooms onto the potatoes, top each dish with a yolk and place in the oven for 7–8 minutes. The potatoes and mushrooms should be hot and the egg yolks starting to blister and cook. Remove from the oven, sprinkle with parsley, season, and serve.

A Trebbiano d'Abbruzo from Italy will complement the smoky mushrooms.

Classic Tortilla

Tortillas are found in every restaurant and every home in Spain, although the quality can vary hugely. It's such a simple dish of only three ingredients: eggs, potatoes and onions, but the technique can take a bit of practice. Super fresh, free-range or organic eggs are a must here along with a good-quality, non-stick pan. With a tortilla, you have the perfect vehicle for your favourite ingredients. Try tossing asparagus, ham, grated cheese, diced peppers or chopped, fresh herbs through the egg mix before cooking for great variations.

Serves 4–6 as part of a main or 8–10 as a starter or tapa

A non-stick, ovenproof frying pan, 25cm in diameter and about 5cm deep

7 medium King Edward or Chipper's Choice potatoes, peeled, sliced thinly (a mandoline or food processor is useful for this)

5 medium Spanish onions, peeled, cut in half, very thinly sliced

8, maybe 9, large, free-range or organic eggs, thoroughly whisked in a bowl

olive oil for cooking

1 litre vegetable oil for frying

sea salt and black pepper

Preheat the oven to 200°C.

In a saucepan, heat a lug of olive oil over a medium heat and add the onions. Season and cook until the onions are very soft but not coloured. Remove the onions from the pan, drain in a colander and reserve. Wash the potatoes under cold water, drain and dry well. Heat the vegetable oil until a piece of potato fizzles but doesn't colour when dropped into a deep-sided saucepan or to 140°C in a deep fat fryer. In 2 or 3 batches, fry the potatoes for about 10 minutes until cooked through but with little colour. Transfer the potatoes onto kitchen paper to drain.

Mix together the potatoes and onions and season. Stir in the beaten eggs and mix well. The mix shouldn't be too dry: there should be some movement of the egg when the bowl's shaken. If not, add another egg.

Heat the frying pan over a medium heat and add a lug of oil. When hot, add the tortilla mix and press down into the pan so it's evenly spread with a slight mound in the middle. Cook for 3–4 minutes over a high heat. Then transfer the pan to the oven to cook for a further 12–15 minutes, or until the top has sealed but there's still a spring when pressed with a finger. Don't let the middle of the tortilla set completely: a knife inserted into the centre will come out piping hot and with some runny egg on it when the tortilla's done. Rest for a few minutes before turning out onto a dish. Cut into slices and sprinkle with sea salt.

Try a spicy Rosso di Montalcino from Tuscany.

Patatas Fritas

With Romesco & Alioli

This is our Spanish take on the all-time classic: chips with ketchup and mayonnaise. We twice-cook the chips in olive oil to impart a rich flavour, and then finish with our smoked paprika sea salt, a dollop of garlicky alioli and a piquant romesco sauce. They're irresistibly moreish, especially when served alongside the Ibérico pork burger. Use King Edward or Maris Piper potatoes for the chips and they'll turn out crispy on the outside and fluffy inside.

Serves 4 as a side or

6–8 as a tapa

A deep fat fryer or thermometer is recommended for this recipe

5 large Maris Piper or King Edward potatoes, peeled, cut into pencil-thin chips

2 litres good-quality olive oil for blanching and cooking

2 tablespoons sea salt

1 tablespoon sweet smoked paprika

100ml alioli (see Basics)

100ml romesco sauce (see Basics)

Make the smoked paprika salt by mixing the paprika and sea salt together.

Place the chips in cold water and turn over a few times to get rid of the starch. Drain the chips well and pat dry on clean kitchen paper. They need to be absolutely dry, otherwise they'll spit in the hot oil.

Heat the olive oil to 130°C in a deep fat fryer or until a single chip dropped into a deep-sided pan fizzles slightly but does not colour. Cook in 2 batches. Lower each batch into the oil and cook for about 7 minutes until nice and tender. Remove the chips from the oil and cool down.

Now the double cooking! Turn the temperature up to 175°C on the fryer or heat the oil in the pan until a chip browns quickly when dropped in. In 2 batches, carefully lower the chips into the oil and cook until crisp and golden brown. Drain well on kitchen paper.

Place the chips in a mixing bowl, sprinkle with the smoked paprika salt and toss well. Divide the chips between individual serving bowls or transfer to a large dish and serve with the alioli and romesco on the side.

Teroldego, an indigenous grape from Northern Italy is little known but delicious with the paprika element of the dish.

PUDDINGS

When it comes to the end of the meal at our restaurants, you'll be handed a short pudding menu. It's kept deliberately brief with perhaps only four or five choices, as many of our puddings are highly seasonal, inspired by whatever fruit is at its best that particular month.

Spain and Italy offer an amazing range of fruit throughout the year. Even the dark winter months are brightened by the arrival of citrus fruit. When the days are short, Spain sends us bittersweet Seville oranges and juicy clementines, while fragrant lemons and ruby-fleshed blood oranges come from Italy.

The rest of the year sees a stream of peaches, apricots, cherries, figs and pomegranates – the list is endless. The UK has a great array of seasonal fruit, too. We're one of the most successful growers of apples and pears in the world and have some of the finest berries around, including raspberries, blackberries and our famous strawberries.

When the new season's fruits arrive in our kitchens, their intoxicating aromas and dramatic colours cause a great stir. Our creative juices begin to flow – along with those of the fruit – and some stunning new takes on traditional puddings are born. Classics such as panna cotta or rice pudding are lightened and given a fruity twist with the addition of some poached rhubarb or macerated strawberries. Cheesecake is given an Italian slant by using Caprino Fresco and amaretti for the base, and is served with raspberries alongside. We've even delved into the French dessert repertoire by adding figs and Marcona almonds to the classic tarte tatin and salted praline and buttermilk to the original Limousin pudding, cherry clafoutis.

There's always a chocolate creation on our menus. We insist on using the best quality chocolate. The higher the cocoa content, the richer and deeper the flavour. A baked 70% bitter chocolate ganacha served straight from the oven with warm roasted fruits and a scoop of freshly churned ice cream has got to be one of the most delicious ways to round off a meal. Sometimes a pick-me-up is all that's needed, especially after one too many glasses of sherry. Our deluxe affogato, which is in essence hot coffee and boozy ice cream, will do the job, or you could simply have a coffee with a couple of freshly baked, fennel-scented cantucci biscuits.

We've included some easy-to-prepare recipes here as well as some more advanced ones. When tackling puddings, remember that there isn't much margin for error. Puddings require exact measurements, unlike the more relaxed intuitiveness of the savoury kitchen. A good set of scales would be a useful investment. Most of the puddings here can be prepared in advance, with only a little last-minute attention, leaving you free to enjoy your dinner and your guests.

CHOCOLATE GANACHA

This is one of our best-selling puddings and there would be uproar if it came off the menu! It's important to use the best bitter chocolate you can afford. We use Valrhona or Amedei as they have really interesting, complex flavours and superb texture. This ganacha is cooked for a few minutes in the oven so the outside is lightly baked and the inside is nice and gooey. Serve with cream, mascarpone or ice cream. At the restaurants, we serve it with turrón ice cream and extra pieces of turrón sprinkled on top.

Serves 4

You will need 4 ovenproof ramekins approx. 8cm in diameter

120g good-quality 70% bitter chocolate, cut into chunks

110g unsalted butter

4 whole eggs

3 yolks

75g caster sugar

50g plain flour, sifted

Place the chocolate in a bowl with 100g of the butter and set over a pan of simmering water. Melt the chocolate and butter, mix well and reserve. Whisk together the eggs, yolks and sugar with a hand whisk or electric mixer until doubled in volume, light and airy. Fold the eggs into the chocolate until fully incorporated and then stir in the flour. Use the remaining butter to grease the ovenproof ramekins and then lightly dust with flour. Shake off any excess. Divide the chocolate mix between the 4 dishes and place in the fridge for about 30 minutes.

Meanwhile, preheat the oven to 220°C. Place the ganachas in the oven and cook for 6 minutes or until the outside is quite firm and the inside still molten. Carefully insert a knife into the middle of one to see how done it is, remembering that the residual heat will continue to cook the insides when they are taken out of the oven, so they really won't need much longer than 6 minutes.

Remove from the oven and serve straight away with a scoop of ice cream or a dollop of thick double cream.

Pedro Ximénez from Andalucia is widely available and won't fail.

CALASPARRA RICE PUDDING BRULÉE

Nobody does rice pudding like the Spanish. Calasparra is a wonderful, nutty, short grain pudding rice hailing from Valencia that absorbs all the flavours of its cooking companions but doesn't turn to mulch. It also makes wonderful risottos and paellas. We add a crunchy caramel top for texture. This is perfect for a dinner party as the rice pudding can be cooked, plated and stored in advance, ready to be caramelised before serving. Try with a scoop of one of our delicious ice creams – the sweet and tart rhubarb one works perfectly.

Serves 4

For the rice pudding:

250g Calasparra short grain rice or pudding rice

150g caster sugar

750ml full cream milk

250ml water

1 vanilla pod, split lengthwise, seeds scraped out and reserved

½ cinnamon stick

zest of 1 lemon

For the brulée:

extra caster sugar

Place all the rice pudding ingredients in a large saucepan, including the vanilla seeds, pod and cinnamon stick, and cook over a medium heat. Bring to the boil and then turn down to a very low heat and simmer for about 40 minutes, or until the rice is cooked and the liquid has been absorbed. Ensure the rice is not too dry. If this is the case, add a splash of milk to moisten lightly.

When the rice is ready, remove the cinnamon stick and vanilla pod, and divide between 4 individual flameproof or ovenproof serving dishes. The puddings can either be bruléed and served straight away, or set aside for later and put in the fridge. If set aside, the rice will be eaten cool and the caramel hot, providing a nice contrast.

To make the caramel top, sprinkle the pudding liberally with caster sugar to cover the rice completely with a good, thickish layer. Either place under a preheated grill or use a blowtorch to achieve a dark caramel. Serve immediately.

A rich, smoky sweet pudding wine from Pantelleria, an island south of Sicily.

COLD CHOCOLATE FONDANT
WITH HONEY ICE CREAM & HONEYCOMB

Another chocolate classic, this is the perfect make-ahead dessert that wows every time with its delicious mousse-like exterior and oozing honey-and-cream centre. Everything can be prepared in advance, allowing you time to entertain. The honeycomb has got to be tried. It adds wonderful crunch to this dish and can be made in larger batches and stored for future use. Try it crumbled onto ice creams or with fresh, seasonal berries. Use our honey ice cream recipe or buy a good-quality one. Vanilla, cinnamon or coffee ice cream would also work well.

Serves 4

You will need 4 x 7–8cm diameter metal rings for this recipe

For the fondant:

180g good-quality 70% bitter chocolate, cut into even chunks

80g caster sugar

2 whole eggs

2 egg yolks

250ml double cream

4 scoops honey ice cream (see Ice Creams & Sorbets)

For the honeycomb:

20g good-quality runny honey

1 tablespoon water

100g caster sugar

35g glucose syrup

5g bicarbonate of soda

To make the honeycomb, it's important to measure out the ingredients as accurately as possible. Place the honey, water, sugar and glucose in a high-sided saucepan and heat over a very high heat. Cook until the liquid turns into a rich, golden syrup or until the temperature reaches 135°C when checked with a sugar thermometer. Immediately, stir in the bicarbonate of soda and transfer the mix to a tray lined with greaseproof paper, allowing it to spread out. Cool completely before use.

To make the fondants, firstly, melt the chocolate in a bowl over a pan of simmering water. Remove from the heat. Now, lightly whip the double cream to form soft peaks. Next, make sugar syrup by putting the sugar in a small sauce-pan with a splash of water and boiling over a high heat until the sugar dissolves. Now you'll combine everything. Put the yolks and eggs in a mixing bowl and whisk rapidly with a hand whisk or electric mixer. While mixing, gradually pour in the sugar syrup until it's fully incorporated and the eggs are light, airy and fluffy. Fold this mix into the melted chocolate, and then fold in the whipped cream. Be careful to fold lightly so as not to knock out too much air but still making sure everything is properly incorporated.

Place the 4 rings on a tray lined with greaseproof paper. Spoon the chocolate mix into the rings so they are a third full, ensuring there are no air gaps. Put in the fridge for 10 minutes or so. Remove the rings from the fridge and place a small scoop of ice cream on top of the chocolate in each ring. Quickly spoon the rest of the chocolate on top of the ice cream so the scoop is completely encased in

chocolate. This is vital otherwise the ice cream will leak. Smooth the top of the rings to neaten things up and transfer to the fridge for at least 2 hours.

When ready to serve, turn out the fondants onto serving plates, warming the outside of the ring with a hot cloth so each fondant is released easily. Sprinkle some broken honeycomb over each fondant and serve with a drizzle of honey, if you like.

Nocino, the sweet dark liqueur made from walnuts, will be perfect with this.

ORANGES POACHED IN CARAMEL

WITH PISTACHIOS, MINT & YOGHURT

A lovely simple pudding that's a perfect finish to a meal, especially when you're not in the mood for one of our more serious desserts. There's a Moorish feel to this dish of caramelised oranges with its bright green pistachios, tangy yoghurt and fragrant mint. It'd be easy to transport yourself to far off climes eating this on a warm summer's eve. Choose a good, thick, organic Greek or natural yoghurt – all the better to dollop with. Try to find unsalted, shelled Iranian pistachios which are superb.

Serves 4

4 large sweet oranges, with not too much pith

200g caster sugar

180ml boiling water

40g fresh pistachios, unsalted and shelled, roughly chopped

1 large handful mint leaves, roughly shredded

250ml Greek-style yoghurt

With a sharp knife, trim the top and bottom off each orange and then cut the skin and pith off in a downward, angled motion so as to cut around the natural shape of the oranges. Take your time with this: a carefully peeled and shaped orange will add greatly to the final presentation. When the oranges are peeled, slice each one horizontally into 7 or 8 rounds and remove any seeds.

To make the caramel, heat the sugar in a large non-stick sauté pan over a medium heat. Shake the pan occasionally while the sugar's cooking to ensure it colours evenly and that all the sugar dissolves. Don't stir the sugar though, as the spoon will stick and the sugar crystallise. When the sugar has fully dissolved into a golden brown caramel, slowly pour in the boiling water, taking great care as the caramel will spit. Stir so that the caramel dissolves into the water – still over a medium heat. When you have a smooth viscous caramel, add the orange slices and swirl the pan to coat them. Turn the heat down to low and cook lightly for 2–3 minutes. Turn off the heat and rest for 2 minutes.

Divide the orange slices between serving plates and spoon over the orange-flavoured caramel. Sprinkle with the chopped pistachios and the mint leaves and serve with a good dollop of yoghurt.

A sweet white wine from Priorat has the intensity and nuttiness to match the caramel oranges.

Vanilla Panna Cotta

With Blood Orange Granita

Panna cotta is one of the easiest puddings to make, yet done properly, it's a thing of beauty which causes gasps of delight as it's brought, wobbling, to the table. Panna cotta means 'cooked cream' in Italian and, at its most simple, it is lightly cooked, sweetened cream set with gelatin. Originating in Northern Italy years ago, it was first set with natural fish bone gelatin, which may well have imparted some of its fishiness! Thankfully, times have moved on since and you can now buy leaf or powdered gelatin which has a neutral flavour.

Serves 4

You will need 4 bowls or 4 x 150ml pudding moulds

For the panna cotta:

3½ leaves fast dissolving gelatin

570ml double cream

170ml full cream milk

1 vanilla pod, split lengthwise, seeds scraped out and reserved

180g icing sugar

For the blood orange granita:

300ml blood orange juice or regular orange juice (about 5 oranges)

a squeeze of lemon juice

150ml water

115g caster sugar

To make the panna cotta, first soak the gelatin leaves in cold water until completely softened, then drain and squeeze the gelatin, ensuring there is no water left. Pour the cream and milk into a saucepan and add the vanilla pod and seeds. Place the pan over a medium heat, bring to the boil and take off the heat. Remove the pod and discard. Whisk in the icing sugar and gelatin until both have fully dissolved. Pour the cream into bowls or – for a more professional presentation – into pudding moulds. Transfer the panna cottas to the fridge and chill for at least 2 hours, or until set but with a slight wobble.

To make the granita, pour the orange juice, lemon juice and water into a saucepan and bring to the boil over a medium heat. Remove from the heat and whisk in the sugar until fully dissolved. Pour the granita mix into a plastic container and allow to cool before transferring to the freezer. Check the granita after 30 minutes or so. When it's started to freeze, scrape around the edges of the container with a fork to break up the freezing juices and create 'snow'. Pop back in the freezer and after another 30 minutes, scrape the mix again. Repeat this process until all the granita has been scraped into snow. Keep in the freezer until needed.

To serve, remove the panna cottas from the fridge. If using moulds, dip them into hot water to loosen their contents, invert over plates and carefully turn out the panna cottas. Serve each panna cotta with a scoop of granita on the side.

A Passito from Piedmont has the right sweetness and freshness to match this wonderfully.

Caprino Fresco Cheesecakes
With Raspberries & Amaretti

These simple set cheesecakes are perfect for summer and are great paired with ripe summer fruits or berries. Amaretti biscuits mixed through a traditional digestive base add a lovely Italian twist. We use Caprino Fresco, a very soft, fresh goat's cheese from Italy, but you could use any soft, mild goat's cheese. This recipe is very quick to make and doesn't require any cooking, just a good firm-up in the fridge and the cheesecakes are ready to go. If you're feeling indulgent, splash over a teaspoon of grappa before serving.

Serves 6

You will need 6 x 4.5cm ring moulds

For the base:

150g amaretti biscuits

85g digestive biscuits

85g unsalted butter, melted

For the filling:

150g cream cheese, such as Philadelphia

75g mascarpone

60g Caprino Fresco or soft, fresh, rindless goat's cheese

75g caster sugar

85ml double cream

seeds from ½ vanilla pod

To finish:

1 punnet raspberries

Firstly make the base. Crush the digestives and amaretti biscuits in a clean tea towel with a rolling pin, or pulse in a food processor, until you have a fairly fine crumb. Place in a bowl and pour in the melted butter and mix thoroughly. Place the ring moulds on a tray and divide the biscuit mix between them, pressing it in firmly and evenly with the back of a spoon. Chill in the fridge for 30 minutes or so.

Now make the filling by whisking the double cream in a bowl until it forms stiff peaks. In a separate bowl, use an electric mixer to mix together all the other ingredients for about 2–3 minutes until fully incorporated. Fold the whipped cream into the cheese mix and divide between the ring moulds. It's a good idea to tap each ring firmly to ensure the mix has fully filled the mould and that no air gaps remain. Transfer the cheesecakes to the fridge and chill for a couple of hours, until fully set and slightly firm to the touch.

When done, help release the cheesecakes from their moulds by running a warm cloth around the edge of the ring. Turn out onto serving plates and serve with the raspberries alongside.

A sweet Moscatel sherry from Andalucia would be a delicious accompaniment.

CHERRY & ALMOND PUDDING

WITH SALTED CARAMEL

This is our take on the classic French bistro pudding clafoutis, which is a sweetened batter baked with ripe cherries or other fruit. Here we give the recipe a twist by braising the cherries with a little vinegar to bring out their natural flavour, adding buttermilk to the batter for some acidity, and finishing with a crunchy topping of salted, almond caramel. Summer is the time for cherries, grown the world over – in the UK we produce some delicious sweet-sour varieties. Out of season, substitute plums, apricots or peaches.

Serves 6–8

You will need 6 x 9cm-diameter ramekins or a large ovenproof or terracotta dish

For the pudding:

125g caster sugar

55g flour, sifted

170ml buttermilk

50ml double cream

a pinch of baking powder

2 large eggs

600g cherries, stones removed

60g caster sugar

1 tablespoon Cabernet Sauvignon vinegar or other red wine vinegar

20g unsalted butter

extra caster sugar for dusting

For the almond caramel:

30g caster sugar

2 tablespoons flaked, toasted almonds

a pinch of sea salt

a squeeze of lemon juice

Preheat the oven to 200°C. To make the batter, place the sugar, flour, buttermilk, cream, baking powder and eggs in a blender and process for 2–3 minutes until smooth. Put the batter in a bowl and rest in the fridge for 25 minutes.

Meanwhile, put the cherries in a saucepan with the sugar and vinegar and place over a medium heat. Simmer the cherries for about 15–20 minutes or until the sugar and juices from the cherries have created a rich syrup and the cherries have cooked down. The time for cooking the cherries will depend on how ripe they are.

For the caramel, heat the sugar in a small saucepan over a medium heat and carefully cook until you achieve a golden caramel. Now add the almonds, salt and lemon juice, stir once and then pour into a baking tray lined with baking parchment. Let the caramel fully cool until hard and brittle and then chop into very small pieces.

Butter and lightly flour the ramekins or baking dish. Divide the cherries and cherry syrup between the dishes and then pour the batter on top. Place on a baking tray and bake for 25–30 minutes or until the batter has risen and started to brown. Remove from the oven to cool.

Sprinkle the almond caramel pieces over the puddings and then caramelise by placing under a hot grill for about 5 minutes. Serve with some ice cream on the side.

Marsala is sweet and nutty, just like this pudding, so will match wonderfully.

Caramelised Fig Tarts

This is our take on the tarte tatin, the classic French upside-down tart loaded with rich, caramelised fruit. Figs are in season in the late summer and early autumn. When selecting your fruit, buy the firmer figs as you'll be cooking them in caramel and then baking and if the figs are overly ripe, there's a danger they'll collapse. At the restaurants, we make individual tartlets but you could, of course, make a large tart to share. These tarts are scrumptious served with our salted Marcona almond ice cream.

Serves 4

You will need 4 x 12cm non-stick tart pans

160g good-quality puff pastry

40g unsalted butter

100g soft dark brown sugar

6 firm figs, cut in half lengthwise

1 stick cinnamon, cut into 4

1 egg, beaten, for egg wash

Preheat the oven to 220°C.

Roll out the puff pastry to a thickness of about 3mm and cut out 4 circles, large enough to fit the tart pans with some overlap. Transfer to the fridge and rest for at least 15 minutes.

Slice the butter thinly and divide between the tart pans. Spoon in the brown sugar. Place 3 fig halves, flesh side down, in each pan and press down into the sugar. Nestle a piece of cinnamon in between the figs. Place the pans in the oven and cook for 10 minutes to caramelise the butter and sugar, aiming for a golden caramel colour. Remove the pans from the oven and allow to cool down completely. Turn the oven down to 200°C.

When cool, place a pastry disc over each tart pan and press around the sides of the figs to encase. Brush each pastry disc with egg wash and prick very lightly with the tip of a knife 5 or 6 times. This will help release any steam during the cooking process. Pop the tarts back in the oven. Cook for 11–12 minutes or until the pastry is crisp and golden brown and the caramel is bubbling around the edges. Remove from the oven and allow to cool for a minute. Carefully turn out the tarts onto serving plates. Serve with a scoop of ice cream or a dollop of cream.

A Moscato d'Asti from Piedmont in Northern Italy is a light, sweet sparkling wine that's a delight with this tart.

SWEET LEMON DOUGHNUTS

WITH SAFFRON CUSTARD

These little doughnuts are a fun way to end a meal and are great for sharing. Everyone can grab a doughnut and dip it into the saffron custard. Rosquillos, or ring doughnuts, along with the more common churros are eaten all over Spain with great enthusiasm. The Spanish like to have them for breakfast with chocolate sauce and a strong coffee. We've created a deep yellow dipping sauce flavoured with saffron threads that works harmoniously with the hot fried, lemon-scented doughnuts. A great end to a dinner – or try them for breakfast!

Makes 30 doughnuts

For the doughnuts:

125ml double cream

1 egg

75g caster sugar and extra for dusting

65ml olive oil

2 tablespoons lemon juice, freshly squeezed

100ml orange juice, freshly squeezed

450g self-raising flour, sifted

zest of 1 lemon

2 litres vegetable oil for deep-frying

For the saffron custard:

300ml double cream

2 pinches saffron threads

4 free-range egg yolks

50g caster sugar

In a bowl, whisk together the cream, eggs and sugar until light and airy. Next whisk in the olive oil, followed by the lemon and orange juice. Finally, fold in the flour, ensuring everything is well mixed. Leave the dough to rest in the fridge for 3 hours. After this, divide the dough into 6 and roll each piece into a long strip with the thickness of a 1-pound coin. Cut these into 5cm strips. Mould each strip around your middle 3 fingers and seal the ends by pressing together. Place the doughnuts on a tray lined with greaseproof paper and rest in the fridge for 20 minutes.

To make the custard, place the cream and saffron in a saucepan and bring slowly to the boil. Remove from the heat and let the saffron infuse. In a bowl, whisk together the yolks and sugar until pale and fluffy, and then gradually whisk in the saffron-infused cream. Pour the mix back into the saucepan and cook gently over a low heat to thicken. Stir constantly to prevent the sauce from curdling. The custard should be thick enough to coat a wooden spoon.

Heat the oil in a high-sided saucepan to approximately 170°C or until a bit of dough browns when dropped in. Slide in the doughnuts, 4 or 5 at a time, and fry until they rise, golden brown, to the surface. Turn them over and cook the other side. The doughnuts should feel fairly light when they're cooked, but will be denser than regular doughnuts or churros. When they're ready, lift out, drain on kitchen paper and toss in caster sugar. Pile on a serving dish, sprinkle with lemon zest and serve with the saffron custard.

Enjoy with an artisan Limoncello – delicious!

BAKED HONEY CHEESECAKE

Everybody loves a cheesecake. This unusual, semi-deconstructed version is our take on the baked New York classic. We've separated its parts, sprinkling the cantucci base on top so that it has something of an upside-down appearance. Its gloriously deep rich caramel flavour comes from the inclusion of muscovado sugar and a honey reduction. Mascarpone adds a pleasing underlying acidity. This recipe makes a large cheesecake which will happily serve ten or more people. You could also halve the quantities and use a smaller cake tin or five individual moulds or ramekins.

Serves about 10

You will need 1 cake tin with a sealed base (about 27cm in diameter), or, for half the recipe, 5 dariole moulds or ramekins (about 7cm in diameter)

480g runny honey

150ml double cream

110g muscovado sugar

350g cream cheese

70g caster sugar

3 eggs

seeds of 1 vanilla pod

680g mascarpone

120g good-quality, shop-bought cantucci or homemade (see page 180) crushed to a coarse crumb

To make the honey cream, place the honey in a saucepan over a medium heat and reduce by two thirds. Remove from the heat and stir in the cream. Reserve.

Preheat the oven to 180°C. Butter the cake tin and sprinkle the sugar on the base and sides. Place the tin in a deep-sided baking tray. Next put the cream cheese and caster sugar in a mixing bowl and whisk until soft and creamy. Beat in the eggs, one by one, along with the vanilla seeds. Gently stir in the mascarpone, but only until the lumps disappear. Whisk half of the honey cream into the cheese mix, reserving the rest for later. Transfer the mix to the sugared tin, spread it about evenly, and then pour hot water around the tin to about a third of the way up the sides. Cover the tray with foil and transfer to the oven and cook for about 45 minutes or until the cake is just starting to set and colour. Remove the foil, reduce the temperature to 170°C and cook for a further 30 minutes, or until the cake has started to puff up and there is no sign of any liquid in the centre. Remove from the oven and cool down to room temperature in the water bath. Chill in the fridge for a few hours until the cake is completely set.

When ready to serve, loosen the edges of the cake with a knife and warm the base lightly with a warm cloth to release the bottom. Carefully turn the cake onto a serving plate. Serve with the coarse cantucci crumbs sprinkled on top and the remaining honey cream on the side.

A dessert wine from Priorat in Spain will have the body to work a treat with this cheesecake.

Macerated & Fresh Strawberries

With Mascarpone & Vanilla

There's nothing like the sight and scent of perfectly ripe, red strawberries to get summer spirits soaring. Our take on the quintessentially English classic of strawberries and cream is quick and easy to prepare, making it a great choice of pudding for a spontaneous barbecue or al fresco lunch. In this recipe, we serve some of the strawberries macerated with a little vinegar alongside the fresh ones, for an interesting textural contrast. The black pepper is a great addition: an unlikely but worthwhile partner which brings out the sweetness of the strawberries.

Serves 4

400g seasonal ripe strawberries

2 teaspoons balsamic vinegar

juice and zest of ½ orange

55g caster sugar

2 pinches freshly ground black pepper

100g mascarpone

seeds of ½ vanilla pod

Remove the stalks from the strawberries and cut in half lengthwise – or into quarters, if they're large. Take half the strawberries and place them in a bowl along with the vinegar, orange juice and zest, 30g of the caster sugar and the black pepper. Toss everything together and leave the strawberries to macerate for about 30 minutes in a warm spot, such as near the cooker.

Whisk the mascarpone with the remaining 25g sugar and the vanilla seeds.

Divide the fresh strawberries between serving plates and spoon on the macerated strawberries together with their flavoursome marinating juices. Finish each plate with a scoop of the vanilla mascarpone.

Moscato Rosa is a sweet red from Alto Adige, Northern Italy that's perfect with strawberries.

CHURROS WITH HOT CHOCOLATE SAUCE
& WHIPPED CREAM

Two dishes probably epitomise Spanish cooking above all others – the first, of course, is paella and the second, churros. Anybody who's been to Spain and experienced churros in their hot, sugared glory will testify to their deliciousness. Spaniards eat churros at any time of the day, but especially for breakfast, and we suggest you do the same. There's nothing like dipping cinnamon-spiced doughnuts into melted chocolate to get the day going! You can buy churros makers – or churrerias, as they're called – from homeware shops, if you want to make them regularly.

Makes about 20 churros

For the churros:

120g plain flour, sifted

120g self-raising flour, sifted

a pinch of salt

400ml boiling water

2 tablespoons extra virgin olive oil

vegetable oil for frying

For the chocolate sauce:

200ml full cream milk

40g unsalted butter

300g good-quality 70% bitter chocolate, cut into chunks

To finish:

180g caster sugar

2 tablespoons ground cinnamon

200ml double cream, whipped into soft peaks

First make the batter. Mix together the flours and salt in a bowl and, in a separate bowl, whisk together the boiling water and olive oil. Pour the water and oil into the flour and stir for a minute or so until everything combines together to form a soft, sticky dough. Rest in the fridge for 30 minutes before using.

To make the chocolate sauce, warm the milk in a saucepan over a medium heat and then stir in the butter and chocolate. Carry on cooking and stirring until the chocolate and butter have melted and the sauce is rich and glossy. Reserve, keeping warm. Now make the cinnamon sugar to coat the churros by mixing together the sugar and cinnamon in a bowl.

When the dough has rested, place in a piping bag with a nozzle – or in the churreria – and pipe out 12cm-long fingers of dough onto a tray greased with vegetable oil. Heat the vegetable oil in a deep-sided saucepan till a piece of dough turns brown when dropped in, or in a deep fat fryer to 170°C. Carefully fry the churros in batches for 3 minutes on one side and 2 minutes on the other, or until golden brown. Remove from the oil, drain well on kitchen paper and toss in the cinnamon sugar while they're still hot so the sugar sticks and coats them well. Serve at once with the warm chocolate sauce and a dollop of whipped cream on the side.

This has to be enjoyed with a brandy from Jerez in Spain even at breakfast time. Try to find Cardinal Mendoza – it's great!

ALMOND & FENNEL CANTUCCI

Cantucci biscuits are an Italian end-of-dinner favourite originating from Prato in Tuscany. Also known as biscotti di Prato, the name biscotto points to their double-baking process: bi means 'twice' and cotto means 'cooked'. They're often served with strong espresso or to be dipped in a glass of sweet, amber-coloured Vin Santo. We use almonds and fennel seeds in this recipe, but you could use pistachios or pine nuts instead and vary the spicing with anise or cinnamon. If feeling decadent, why not throw in some little chocolate chunks too?

Makes about 24 cantucci

215g plain flour, sifted

225g whole almonds, cut in half

225g caster sugar

3 teaspoons fennel seeds

2 teaspoons baking powder

20g unsalted butter, melted

2 whole eggs, beaten

2 egg yolks

a little flour for dusting

Preheat the oven to 180°C.

In a large mixing bowl, combine together the flour, almonds, sugar, fennel seeds and baking powder. Gradually mix in the butter and eggs. Mix everything very well. The mix will be quite stiff but this is correct. You may find mixing with your hands easier than with a spoon. Divide the dough in 2 and form 2 even-sized logs. Lightly dust a baking sheet or tray with flour and lay the logs side by side on the tray, making sure to leave a good gap in between as they'll expand in the oven. Bake for 20–25 minutes until light golden on the outside and firm to the touch. Remove from the oven and let the logs cool down to the point when you can touch them without burning your fingers.

Now cut each log at a diagonal angle into 2cm-thick slices. It's important to do this while the log is still warm, as the more it cools down, the more brittle it becomes. You'll end up with broken biscuits, if you cut too late!

Lay the cantucci slices on the baking tray and pop back in the oven for another 10–15 minutes until the biscuits are golden brown and firm. Remove and place on a wire rack. Let the cantucci cool down completely before serving. Alternatively, store in an airtight container for later use. They will keep for about 5 days.

The classic match with this, for good reason, is a Vin Santo from Tuscany.

Pedro Ximénez & Raisin Affogato
With Chocolate & Lemon

Affogato is the ultimate after-dinner pick-me-up. Delicious, homemade ice cream is topped at the last minute with a shot of strong coffee. You don't need much of this: one scoop and you'll be raring to go. We give a Spanish twist to an otherwise Italian dessert by adding sweet, spicy Pedro Ximénez, juicy raisins, a little lemon zest and some grated, bitter chocolate. Traditionally, a shot of espresso is poured over the ice cream, but some good, strong cafetière coffee will do as well.

Serves 4 or more as a pick-me-up

500ml ice cream base
(see Ice Cream & Sorbets)

50ml Pedro Ximénez sherry

60g raisins, chopped roughly

zest of ½ lemon

40g grated bitter chocolate
(70% cocoa)

4 shots of espresso or around
100ml very strong filter coffee
(25ml per serving)

Pour the Pedro Ximénez into a small pan and warm over a low heat. Tip in the chopped raisins and remove the pan from the heat. Leave the raisins to steep for 15 minutes or until the Pedro Ximénez has cooled.

Pour the ice cream base into an ice cream machine and churn. 10 minutes before the ice cream is ready, pour in the raisins and Pedro Ximénez and continue to churn until the ice cream is ready. Now transfer the ice cream to the freezer for at least 1 hour before you serve.

When you are ready to serve, make your coffee. Take the ice cream from the freezer, place 4 large scoops in 4 serving bowls and sprinkle with lemon zest and grated chocolate. Pour the coffee, which must be hot, over the ice cream at the table. Bottoms up!

No wine needed. Enjoy this with an Amaretto on the side.

ICE CREAMS & SORBETS

Our ice cream and sorbet selection evoke the wonderful flavours of Spain and Italy. After you've made your first homemade batch, there'll be no turning back. An ice cream machine is recommended to make quick, smooth, crystal-free ice cream but it is possible to do things by hand, manually churning the ice cream over time as it slowly freezes. All ice cream benefits from sitting at room temperature for 15 minutes or so before serving.

ICE CREAM BASE

Makes 500ml

250ml double cream

250ml full cream milk

125g caster sugar

8 free-range egg yolks

Pour the milk and cream into a saucepan, bring slowly to the boil and then remove from the heat.

In a mixing bowl, whisk together the sugar and yolks for 2–3 minutes until the sugar has dissolved and the yolks are pale and airy.

Pour a little of the milk and cream mix into the sweetened yolks and whisk well. Now pour this yolk mixture into the pan of milk and cream and whisk well. Return the pan to a low heat and stir with a wooden spoon. Lightly cook the base without scrambling the egg. Stir continually until the custard becomes thick enough to coat the back of your spoon. This will take about 7 minutes or so.

Remove the base from the heat and cool for 15 minutes or so. It is now ready to be churned in a machine until frozen, or put in a container in the freezer, removing every now and again to churn by hand until you are happy with the consistency.

MARCONA ALMOND

Makes about 500ml

500ml ice cream base

50g salted Marcona almonds, roughly chopped

Churn the ice cream base in the ice cream machine or by hand. 5 minutes before the ice cream is ready, add the chopped almonds and finish churning. Transfer to the freezer until needed.

TURRÓN

Makes about 500ml

500ml ice cream base

75g soft turrón

75g hard turrón, chopped

Turrón is a lovely Spanish nougat which you will find in many delis. Put the ice cream base into an ice cream machine and churn, or churn by hand. 10 minutes before the ice cream is ready, add the soft turrón and ensure it's properly distributed through the base. 2 minutes before the ice cream is ready, add the hard turrón. Finish churning and then transfer to the freezer until ready to serve.

Rhubarb

Makes about 500ml

500ml ice cream base

200g new season's rhubarb, chopped

40g caster sugar

Start to churn the ice cream base in a machine or by hand in the freezer. Place the rhubarb and sugar in a saucepan and place over a medium heat. Cook the rhubarb for 15 minutes or until the rhubarb has broken down and the sugar has dissolved into the fruit juices. 5 minutes before the ice cream base is fully churned, add the cooked rhubarb and continue to churn until firm. Transfer to the freezer until needed.

Salted Caramel

Makes about 500ml

170g caster sugar

325ml double cream

150ml full cream milk

4 egg yolks

1 teaspoon sea salt, or to taste

Place 100g of the caster sugar in a small saucepan and place over a high heat until the sugar starts to bubble and turn dark brown around the edges. Turn the heat down to medium and give the pan a little shake to ensure there is an even distribution of heat. Do not be tempted to stir the caramel, as it will stick and crystalise.

When the sugar has turned a deep, rich caramel colour, pour in the cream and bring to the boil. When the caramel has all dissolved in the cream,

add the milk, mix well and turn off the heat. Whisk the remaining sugar and eggs in a mixing bowl until light, pale and fluffy. Pour the hot caramel cream gradually into the yolk mix and whisk to incorporate.

Pass the ice cream mix through a sieve into a container and cool down completely before sprinkling with Maldon salt. Churn the ice cream in a machine or by hand until firm and smooth.

Caramelised Milk

Makes about 1 litre

1 litre full cream milk

135g condensed milk

25g caster sugar

Pour the condensed milk into a medium-sized bowl and reserve.

Place the milk and sugar in a medium-sized saucepan and place over a medium heat. Bring slowly to the boil, stirring as you go so the milk doesn't stick. When the milk boils, lower the heat to a simmer and reduce the milk by half. Keep an eye on the milk as it reduces to make sure it doesn't burn. When the milk has reduced, pour it onto the condensed milk and whisk to fully combine.

Let the milk mix cool down completely before churning in an ice cream machine or by hand until firm and smooth. Transfer to the freezer until ready to use.

HONEY

Makes about 500ml

500ml ice cream base

50ml blossom honey

Churn the ice cream base in an ice cream machine or by hand. 5 minutes before the churning process is complete, add the honey. Continue to churn and then transfer to the freezer until required.

STRAWBERRY & MASCARPONE

Makes around 500ml

200g fresh, very ripe strawberries, stalks removed, cut into pieces

250ml milk

4 free-range egg yolks

125g caster sugar

250g full cream mascarpone

Place the strawberries in a blender and blend to a fine purée. Pass the strawberry purée through a sieve and reserve until you are ready to use.

Pour the milk into a saucepan and bring to the boil over a medium heat. Remove the pan from the heat as soon as the milk has boiled.

Whisk together the egg yolks and sugar until light, pale and fluffy. Then gradually pour in the hot milk, whisking as you go. Do not add the milk too quickly, or it may scramble the eggs. When the milk and eggs are fully blended, transfer to a saucepan and heat very slowly over a medium heat, stirring with a wooden spoon. Now, cook the cream mixture until thick enough to coat the back of the spoon. When ready, remove the pan from the heat and cool for 15 minutes or so before whisking in the mascarpone until fully incorporated. Now whisk in the strawberry purée. Churn in an ice cream machine or manually in the freezer.

APRICOT & THYME SORBET

Makes about 800ml–1 litre

250g semi-dried apricots

2 teaspoons fresh thyme leaves, roughly chopped

750ml boiling water

1 egg white, beaten lightly

juice of 1 lemon

For the stock syrup:

170g sugar

170ml water

a squeeze of lemon

Make the stock syrup by placing the sugar and water in a small pan over a high heat. Bring to the boil and then simmer for 3 minutes to dissolve the sugar. Add a squeeze of lemon juice and reserve.

Place the apricots in a medium-sized saucepan along with the thyme and the boiling water. Leave the apricots to soak for 30 minutes or so and then place the pan on a high heat and bring to the boil. Cook the apricots for 20–25 minutes until very soft and tender. Remove from the water. Pass the water through a sieve to extract the thyme leaves. Place the apricots and the strained water in a blender and process to a smooth purée. Now add the lemon juice and stock syrup and blend again to combine everything together. Let the mix cool down before pouring into an ice cream machine and churning or churn by hand for about 15 minutes, before adding the egg white. The egg white will keep the sorbet smooth and soft. Continue to churn the sorbet until set and then transfer to the freezer until ready to use.

FINO SORBET

Makes about 1 litre

500ml Fino

375g caster sugar

juice of 1 lemon

In a medium-sized saucepan, cook the Fino, lemon juice and sugar over a medium heat until they come to the boil and the sugar has dissolved.

Remove from the heat and let the syrup cool down completely before churning in an ice cream machine or by hand. Transfer the sorbet to the freezer until ready to use.

BITTER CHOCOLATE & GRAPPA SORBET

Makes about 800ml

150g best-quality 70% bitter cocoa powder, such as Valrhona or Amedei

400g caster sugar

75ml grappa or another strong, white spirit

750ml water

1 pinch Maldon salt

Place the water and sugar in a saucepan, bring to the boil and make a syrup. Remove from the heat and cool for 5 minutes before whisking in the grappa. Pour the syrup over the cocoa powder and whisk until thoroughly combined.

Ensure the mixture is cold and then add the salt. Churn in an ice cream machine or by hand until firm and smooth and then transfer to a freezer until ready to use.

BASICS

ALIOLI

Makes about 200ml

1 large free-range egg yolk

½ clove garlic, peeled, very finely chopped

1 small teaspoon Dijon mustard

100ml vegetable oil

100ml extra virgin olive oil

white wine vinegar, to taste

lemon juice, to taste

sea salt and black pepper

This is the Spanish version of mayonnaise. Delicious as is or it can be easily souped up by adding herbs, orange zest, paprika or even squid ink.

Place the yolk in a mixing bowl along with the mustard and the garlic. Begin whisking and slowly add the oils to emulsify with the yolk. As the oils incorporate into the yolk, you can speed up the process. When all the oil has been added, season with salt and pepper and add lemon juice and vinegar to taste.

VINAIGRETTE

Makes about 1 litre

250ml Moscatel vinegar, red wine vinegar or white balsamic vinegar

1 teaspoon Dijon mustard

750ml extra virgin olive oil

table salt and black pepper

This is a classic vinaigrette. We use Moscatel vinegar for ours to add a Spanish touch.

In a large bowl, whisk together the vinegar and mustard and then gently whisk in the olive oil until emulsified. Season with salt and pepper and then pour into a bottle or jar. Give the vinaigrette a good shake each time before use to re-emulsify the ingredients. The dressing will last about 1 month in the fridge.

CLASSIC TOMATO SAUCE

Makes about 500ml

500g fresh plum tomatoes, stalk and eye removed, roughly chopped

400g good-quality tinned plum tomatoes, roughly chopped

1 small onion, peeled, sliced

3 cloves garlic, peeled, sliced

1 handful fresh basil, roughly chopped

olive oil for cooking

sea salt and black pepper

Use this sauce for fresh pasta, braising meatballs or as a stand-alone sauce with grilled meats or fish.

Heat a medium-sized saucepan over a medium heat and add a good lug of olive oil. Add the onion and garlic and cook until softened and lightly browned. Now add all the tomatoes and season well. Cook for about 30 minutes until the tomatoes have broken down and the sauce thickened. Turn off the heat, then stir the basil leaves into the sauce. Leave the sauce to settle for about 20 minutes before using.

ROMESCO SAUCE

Makes about 500ml

4 red peppers, quartered, deseeded

10 tomatoes, halved, stalks removed

2 red chillies, halved lengthwise

10 sundried tomatoes in olive oil

4 cloves garlic, peeled

100ml red wine

100ml red wine vinegar

200ml extra virgin olive oil

(such as Arbequina)

extra olive oil for cooking

sea salt and black pepper

Our take on the Spanish classic. Just add some finely chopped almonds and hazelnuts for a more authentic version. It's brilliant as a dip for patatas fritas or served with grilled fish.

Preheat the oven to 190°C. Place the peppers, tomatoes, chilli, garlic and sundried tomatoes on an oven tray and sprinkle with olive oil, salt and pepper. Place the tray in the oven and roast for 40 minutes, until the vegetables are cooked and starting to caramelise. Turn the oven down to 170°C and continue to cook for about another 40 minutes, or until the natural vegetable juices have started to evaporate and the vegetables have caramelised further. Remove the tray from the oven and transfer the vegetables to a bowl. Pour the vinegar and wine into the roasting tray and deglaze over a hob burner, scraping up all the sediment and stirring till it dissolves into the liquid. Pour the vinegary wine over the vegetables and leave to infuse for 15 minutes. Tip everything into a food processor or blender and turn onto high. Blitz the vegetables whilst slowly adding the extra virgin olive until you have a smooth, emulsified purée. Pass through a sieve if desired, and then season to taste.

AJO BLANCO

Serves 4 as a soup

250g whole, blanched almonds

4 cloves garlic, very finely chopped

725ml cold water

100g day-old white bread, crusts removed, ripped into small pieces

2 tablespoons extra virgin olive oil

3 tablespoons Moscatel vinegar or white balsamic vinegar

sea salt and black pepper

A refreshing white gazpacho which can be served chilled as a refreshing soup, or spooned over grilled meats and fish for a garlic hit.

Place the bread in a bowl, pour over a little cold water and soak for 15 minutes. Place the almonds in a food processor and blend until you have a fine powder. Now pour in 200ml of the water and continue to blend until you have a loose paste. Add the garlic and blend for a further 2 minutes. Drain the bread and add it to the almond paste along with the vinegar and olive oil. Continue to blend, slowly adding the rest of the water. When the water is fully incorporated, season the ajo blanco and then transfer to the fridge for at least an hour before serving.

Truffle Honey

500g blossom honey

1 teaspoon black truffles (fresh, tinned or frozen), finely chopped

1 teaspoon brandy

2 teaspoons white truffle oil

Truffle honey goes perfectly with hard, salty cheeses such as Parmesan and Pecorino. You could also stir a spoonful into ice cream for a luxurious finish.

Pour the honey into a saucepan and place the pan over a low heat. Gently warm the honey through and then add the brandy, truffle oil and chopped black truffles. Leave the honey on a very low heat for about 15 minutes to infuse and then transfer into a clean, sealable container. The honey does not need to be refrigerated and will last for up to 3 months.

Red Onion Marmalade

Makes about 100g

3 medium red onions, peeled, finely sliced

1 heaped tablespoon demerara sugar

2 tablespoons Cabernet Sauvignon vinegar or other red wine vinegar

olive oil for cooking

sea salt and black pepper

Works with most salty cheeses and delicious with grilled meats, like our Ibérico pork burger.

Heat a medium-sized saucepan over a medium heat. Add a lug of olive oil and then the onions, sugar and seasoning. Cook the onions for about 40–50 minutes until they've fully softened and have started to caramelise. Stir from time to time to make sure they don't stick. When the onions are ready, add the vinegar and cook for a further 5–6 minutes or until the vinegar has evaporated. When ready, the onions should have a jam-like consistency with a sweet-and-sour flavour.

Salsa Verde

Makes about 550ml

1 bunch flat-leaf parsley leaves

1 bunch basil leaves

1 bunch mint leaves

350ml extra virgin olive oil

40g miniature pickled capers

2 salted anchovies (optional)

juice of ½ lemon

sea salt and black pepper

A punchy, vibrant, herb-loaded sauce, that's equally at home with grilled meats, fish, pasta or vegetables.

Place all the leaves in a blender or food processor and then add the capers, anchovies if using, and half of the olive oil. Switch on and gradually add the rest of the oil until it's fully incorporated and the herbs are finely blended. You should have a thick sauce. Season the salsa and then add the lemon juice. This will keep well in the fridge for up to 10 days.

FISH STOCK

Makes about 3 litres

1.2kg white fish bones, cleaned, rinsed, cut into pieces

2 leeks

2 sticks celery

1 large white onion

1 head fennel

400ml dry white wine

2 bay leaves

1 teaspoon black peppercorns

1 bunch parsley stalks

4 litres cold water

This quick and simple recipe will give you a full-flavoured stock that's not overpowering.

Heat a medium-sized saucepan over a medium heat, add a lug of olive oil and the fish bones and cook until they have turned white and opaque. Now add the onion, fennel, celery and leeks and cook slowly for a few minutes without colouring. Next add the wine, bay, peppercorns and parsley stalks. Bring the wine to the boil and reduce down to a glaze.

Pour in the water and bring to the boil. Lower the heat and skim off any impurities that rise to the surface. Simmer the stock for 40 minutes, skimming as you go. Then turn off the heat and leave the stock to stand for 1 hour before passing through a sieve into a container. The stock is now ready to use.

DARK CHICKEN STOCK

Makes about 3 litres

1.5kg chicken bones

2 carrots, peeled, roughly chopped

1 onion, peeled, cut in half

2 sticks celery, chopped

½ head garlic

1 bay leaf

½ teaspoon black peppercorns

1 tablespoon tomato purée

250ml red wine

4 litres cold water

olive oil for cooking

Nothing beats a fresh, homemade chicken stock. This classic recipe forms the base for many sauces, soups and braises.

Preheat the oven to 200°C. Place the chicken bones in a deep-sided roasting tray and roast until golden brown. Remove the bones from the tray and set aside. Carefully pour away any fat. Pour the wine into the tray and place over a high heat on the hob. Deglaze, scraping the tray with a wooden spoon to release any sediment from the bottom. Reduce the wine by half.

Meanwhile, place a stock pan over a medium heat and add a lug of olive oil. Throw in the vegetables, bay, peppercorns and garlic and cook for 5–8 minutes, stirring as you go. When the vegetables are browned, add the tomato paste and cook for 2 minutes. Pour the reduced wine from the roasting tray into the stock pan of browned vegetables and then add the chicken bones. Pour in enough cold water to cover the bones by at least 5cm. Bring the water to the boil and skin off any scum or impurities that rise to the surface.

When the stock has boiled for 5 minutes, lower the heat and cook at a simmer for about 3 hours, skimming the stock from time to time. Pass the liquid through a fine mesh sieve and it's ready to use.

VEGETABLE STOCK
Makes about 1 litre

2 carrots, peeled, roughly chopped

2 onions, peeled, quartered

2 stalks celery, roughly chopped

½ bulb fennel, roughly chopped

stalk from a head of broccoli, roughly chopped

2 tomatoes

6 black peppercorns

1 dried bay leaf

3 fresh parsley stalks

1.5 litres cold water

This light, fragrant stock can be used for meat, fish and vegetable-based dishes.

Place all the ingredients in a large saucepan and pour over the cold water. Set the pan over a high heat and bring to the boil. When the stock is boiling, turn down to a simmer and cook slowly for 35–40 minutes, skimming off any scum or impurities that rise to the surface with a ladle. Turn off the heat and leave the stock to cool to room temperature before straining through a sieve. The stock is now ready to use.

OLIVE OIL MASH
Serves 4 as a side

4 large or 6 medium Désirée or Rooster potatoes, peeled, evenly diced

200ml double cream

120g unsalted butter, diced

160ml extra virgin olive oil

table salt and white pepper

Our indulgent olive oil mash is popular at the restaurant, with slow-cooked meat, grilled fish, crispy poached eggs or sautéed mushrooms.

Place the potatoes in a saucepan, cover with cold water, add salt and bring to the boil over a high heat. Once boiling, reduce the heat and cook the potatoes at a simmer until they are tender. Drain well and then return the potatoes to the saucepan over a low heat. Shake the pan and let the potatoes steam to release any excess moisture. Now mash the potatoes until very smooth and, still over a low heat, gradually whisk in the butter, the cream and the olive oil. Season to taste and serve.

Aphrodisiacal Afterword

By Stephen Bayley

Stephen Bayley is an author, critic, curator and consultant. With Sir Terence Conran, he created London's innovative Design Museum. He is a Dehesa regular.

'Tell me what you eat, and I will tell you what you are' is one of the most resonant truths about people and food. Its author was Jean Anthelme Brillat-Savarin whose 1825 *Physiologie du Goût* has never been surpassed as a study in the psychology of eating. If what we eat affects both our bodies and our minds, it makes sense to pay scrupulous attention to the menu. It would be a mistake not to. Here is the source of all those smutty speculations about aphrodisiacs. The Romans made a direct connection between eating the genitals of animals thought to be notably romantic in inclination (the ass, the wolf and the deer, in their opinion) and a helpfully inflammatory effect below the belt. The Chinese still believe this. And what about the prospect of being turned on by a potato? In Elizabethan England this was a reality: the exotic, rare and expensive potato was held to have impressive venereal powers. Further abroad, the author of *The Perfumed Garden* claimed that a diet of onions would cause an erection lasting a month.

But when the schoolboy sniggering has subsided, there's the satisfyingly deep cultural history of food and sex. The principle of the Slow Food Movement is that only two things are fundamental to the progress of humankind: food and sex. And each is best done slowly. I was told this over lunch by Carlo Petrini, founder of the movement. Petrini, perhaps aware of the potato's erotic reputation, persistently stole the chips off my plate.

There's not much scientific proof for aphrodisiacs. It's more a question of: if you believe in them, they work. Oysters? Perhaps to the imaginative eye an oyster has a certain appearance which might, in the sensitive, have a stimulating effect. And the symbolism continues, you have to prise the oysters open to reveal a delicious secret, soft and yielding...But let's not get carried away. What's really going on is different. The mind leaps from the sense of well-being, created by something as brinily delicious and sensuous as the oyster, to equivalent pleasures located in other zones of the body. It's about intellectual associations, not neurochemicals.

And then there are the surroundings. Our environment affects our taste: an oyster eaten in a Peckham bus stop is a different experience to an oyster eaten while slouching on a schmoozy, claret-coloured, velour banquette in a dark little bistrot in the sixteenth arrondissement. So here is a second important truth about eating to add to Brillat-Savarin's first: tell me where you eat, and I will tell you what you want to be. Restaurants are about much more than food. It's not enough to get you from Vitamin A to Vitamin B: you have to go on an imaginative journey as well. Of course, no-one would want to overlook the importance of proper sourcing and the correct preparation of food, but the kitchen is just one part of the experience a restaurant offers. Restaurants are theatres where you are on stage. You are not paying just for the food and service, you are gaining access to a dreamworld where suggestion and opportunity are in the air. To be successful, a restaurant must offer not only interesting, possibly even aphrodisiacal, food, but also a totally designed

experience in which you are invited, at whatever level you choose, to participate. I have my own candidates for the ultimate in restaurant romance. The Oyster Bar at Manhattan's Grand Central Station, with its destination board a gazetteer of New York suburbia, and all its suggestions of eternal boredom and occult spasmodic eroticism on weekday afternoons. The nautical, wood-panelled Coco Beach in Nice – surely the best view in the world? Miramar in Marseilles Vieux-Port, with bouillabaisse trickling down the chin. A little place with no name in a back street off the Ginza, Tokyo, where they serve snake to the yakuza (and the bold tourist). Piperno in Rome's Ghetto, where even in summer Jewish matrons wear fur coats while eating their carciofi alla giudia.

Writing this is not merely making me feel hungry, it is making me feel...how can I put it? Romantic. This is the effect that good restaurants have. So we return to the notions of consumption, a word which suggests both digestion and desire. Consider that famous old inquiry: 'Are you free for dinner?' This is a question loaded with nuance. If a specific restaurant is mentioned, a declaration of taste has been made to accompany the veiled declaration of lust. McDonald's or Dehesa? This goes deeper. In a pattern that anthropologists recognise, the dinner invitation allows the male to realise the archaic role of provider. For the female guest, there is the more modern moral dilemma: to accept the ultimate implications of dinner after only a cheeseburger and a Diet Coke or hold out for pata negra and a Vega Sicilia 1970? What sort of a woman do you take me for? You see? We're back to the question of tell me what you eat, and I will tell you what you are.

FOOD SHOPS
LONDON

IBÉRICO PORK
Fine Food Specialist
0207 746 2436
www.finefoodspecialist.co.uk
(UK wide delivery)

Freedown Food
0207 720 4520
www.freedownfood.co.uk
(UK wide delivery)

Harrods
87–135 Brompton Road
London SW1X 7XL
0207 730 1234
www.harrods.com

Harvey Nichols
109–125 Knightsbridge
London SW1X 7RJ
0207 235 5000
www.harveynichols.com

Jack 0'Shea Butchers
11 Montpellier Street
London SW7 1EX
0207 581 7771
www.jackosheas.com

SPANISH SPECIALISTS
Brindisa
Brindisa Shop
The Floral Hall
Stoney Street
Borough Market
London SE1 9AF
0207 407 1036
www.brindisa.com/store

Ibérica
Ibérica Marylebone
195 Great Portland Street
London W1W 5PS
0207 636 8650

Ibérica Canary Wharf
12 Cabot Square
London E14 4QQ
0207 636 8650
www.ibericalondon.co.uk

R. Garcia and Sons
248 Portobello Road
London W11 1LL
0207 221 6119
www.rgarciaandsons.com

ITALIAN SPECIALISTS
Gastronomica
Gastronomica Pimlico
45 Tachbrook Street
London SW1V 2LZ
0207 233 6656

Gastronomica Wapping
New Crane Wharf
75 Garnet Street
London E1W 3QS
0207 481 8669
www.gastronomica.co.uk

Giacobazzi's Delicatessen
150 Fleet Road
London NW3 2QX
0207 267 7222
www.giacobazzis.co.uk

I. Camisa & Son
61 Old Compton Street
London W1D 6HS
0207 437 7610
www.icamisa.co.uk

Lina Stores
18 Brewer Street
London W1F 0SH
0207 437 6482
www.linastores.co.uk

Machiavelli Food
Machiavelli Kitchen and
Dining Room
69 Long Acre
London WC2E 9JS
0207 240 2125

Manicomio Chelsea
85 Duke of York Square
London SW3 4LY
0207 730 3366

Manicomio Gutter Lane
6 Gutter Lane
London EC2V 8AS
0207 726 5010
www.machiavellishop.co.uk

Wild Caper
Unit 11a
Brixton Market Row
London SW9 8LB
0207 737 4410
www.wildcaper.co.uk

OUTSIDE LONDON

Good delis which sell
Spanish & Italian products

Appleyards
85 Wyle Cop, Shrewsbury
Shropshire SY1 1UT
01743 240 180

Blasus Deli
58 King Street, Carmarthen
Carmarthenshire SA31 1BD
01267 233 811
www.blasusdeli.co.uk

David Brown Deli
28a Harbour Street
Whitstable
Kent CT5 1DB
01227 274 507

Digey Food Rooms
6 The Digey, St Ives
Cornwall TR26 1HR
01736 799 600
www.digeyfoodroom.co.uk

Estuary Deli
51 The Broadway
Leigh-on-Sea
Essex SS9 1PA
01702 480 384

Hickson & Black's
559a Barlow Moor Road
Chorlton-cum-Hardy
Manchester M21 8AN
01618 812 001
www.hicksonandblacks.co.uk

Hungry Guest Foodstore
Middle Street, Petworth
West Sussex GU28 0BE
01798 342 803
www.thehungryguest.com

Lunya Fusion Deli
18–20 College Lane
Liverpool L1 3DS
01517 069 770
www.lunya.co.uk

Macknade Fine Food
Selling Road, Faversham
Kent ME13 8XF
01795 534 497
www.macknade.com

Papadeli Foods Ltd
84 Alma Road, Clifton
Bristol BS8 2DJ
01179 736 569
http//news.papadeli.co.uk/

Provender Brown
23 George Street
Perth PH1 5JY
Scotland
01738 587 300
www.provenderbrown.co.uk

Quayles
1 Long Street, Tetbury
Gloucestershire GL8 8AA
01666 505 151
www.quayles.co.uk

Relish Food & Drink
Foundry Court, Wadebridge
Cornwall PL27 7QN
01208 814 214
www.relishwadebridge.co.uk

Riverford Farm Foods Ltd
Staverton, Totnes
Devon TQ9 6AF
01803 762 851
www.riverfordfarmshop.co.uk

Roberts & Speight
40 Norwood, Beverley
East Yorkshire HU17 9EY
01482 870 717
www.hamperbox.co.uk

Thyme and Tides
The High Street
Stockbridge, nr Winchester
Hampshire SO20 6HE
01264 810 101
www.thymeandtidesdeli.co.uk

Valvona & Crolla Ltd
19 Elm Row
Edinburgh EH7 4AA
0131 556 6066
www.valvonacrolla.co.uk

WINE SHOPS
LONDON

Askewine
81 Askew Road
London W12 9BJ
0208 746 1585
www.askewine.com

Bedales
5 Bedales Street
Borough Market
London SE1 9AL
0207 403 8853
www.bedaleswines.com

Bottle Apostle
95 Lauriston Road
London E9 7HJ
0208 985 1549
www.bottleapostle.com

Dalla Terra
25 Slingsby Place
St Martin's Courtyard
London WC2E 9AB
0207 240 8811
www.dellaterra.co.uk

Fulham Wine Rooms
871–873 Fulham Road
London SW6 5HP
0207 042 0440
www.greatwinesbytheglass.com

Green and Blue
38 Lordship Lane
London SE22 8HJ
0208 693 9250
www.greenandbluewines.com

Handford Wines
105 Old Brompton Road
London SW7 3LE
0207 589 6113
www.handford.net

Highbury Vintners
71 Highbury Park
London N5 1UA
0207 226 1347
www.highburyvintners.co.uk

Huntsworth Wine Company
108 Kensington Church Street
London W8 4BH
0207 229 1602
www.huntsworthwine.co.uk

Melrose and Morgan
42 Gloucester Avenue
London NW1 8JD
0207 722 0011
www.melroseandmorgan.com

North and South Wines
63 Broomwood Road
London SW11 6HU
0207 228 2431
www.northandsouthwines.co.uk

Planet of the Grapes
9 New Oxford Street
London WC1A 1BA
0207 405 4912
www.planetofthegrapes.co.uk

Robertson Wine
348 Kensington High Street
London W14 8NS
0207 371 2121
www.robertsonwine.co.uk

Jeroboams
0207 288 8850
www.jeroboams.co.uk for
branches in London

Laytons Wine Merchants Ltd
7–9 Elliott's Place, Islington,
London, N1 8HX
0207 288 8850
www.laytons.co.uk

The Good Wine Shop
84 Chiswick High Road
London W4 1SY
0208 994 8184
www.thegoodwineshop.co.uk

Theatre of Wine
75 Trafalgar Road
London SE10 9TS
0208 858 6363
www.theatreofwine.com

OUTSIDE LONDON

Bacchus Wine
38 Market Place, Olney
Bucks MK46 4AJ
01234 711 140
www.bacchus.co.uk

Bentley's Wine Merchants
John Parys House
18 Castle Street, Ludlow
Shropshire SY8 1AT
01584 875 520
www.bentleyswine.com

Buon Vino
The Courtyard, Settle
North Yorks BD24 9JY
01729 892 905
www.buonvino.co.uk

Connolly's Wine Merchants Ltd
379–381 Warwick Road
Olton, Solihull
Birmingham B91 1BQ
0121 709 3734 / 0121 236 9269
www.connollyswine.co.uk

Corks of Cotham
54 Cotham Hill
Bristol BS6 6JX
0117 973 1620
www.corksof.com

Duncan Murray Wines
10 Adam & Eve Street
Market Harborough
Leicestershire LE16 7LT
01858 464 935
www.duncanmurraywines.co.uk

Four Walls Wine Company
Chilgrove, Chichester
West Sussex PO18 9HX
01243 535 353
www.fourwallswine.com

Heaton Wines Ltd
35 Church Street, Romsey
Hampshire SO51 8BT
01790 830 330
www.heaton-wines.com

Joseph Barnes Wines Ltd
13 Market Row
Saffron Walden
Essex CB10 1HB
01799 528 019
www.josephbarneswines.com

New Forest Wine
8 Christchurch Road
Ringwood
Hants BH24 1DN
01425 489 771
www.newforestwine.com

Old Chapel Cellars
The Old Chapel
Millpool, Truro
Cornwall TR1 1EX
01872 270 545
www.oldchapelcellers.co.uk

Regency Wines Ltd
22 Apple Lane
Sowton Industrial Estate
Exeter
Devon EX2 5GL
01392 444 123
www.regencywines.co.uk

Symposium Wine Emporium
32 Lansdown Place, Lewes
East Sussex BN7 2JU
01273 478 933
www.symposium-finewine.co.uk

The Dorset Wine Co
37 Peverell Avenue West
Poundbury, Dorchester
Dorset DT1 3SU
01305 266 734
www.dorsetwine.co.uk

The Oxford Wine Company
The Wine Warehouse
Standlake, Witney
Oxon OX29 7PR
01865 301 144
www.oxfordwine.co.uk

The Solent Cellar
40 St Thomas Street
Lymington SO41 9ND
01590 674 852
www.thesolentcellar.co.uk

The Village Vine
23 Bournemouth Road
Lower Parkstone
Poole BH14 0EF
01202 739 394
www.thevillagevine.co.uk

Vinea
Unit B7, Britannia Pavilion
Albert Dock
Liverpool L3 4AD
0151 707 8962
www.vinealiverpool.co.uk

Wadebridge Wines
The Piazza
Eddystone Road
Wadebridge
Cornwall PL27 7AL
01208 812 692
www.waderbridgewines.co.uk

Ben Tish

Firstly to HELEN DRIVER, DAVID DRIVER and JASON LOWE for making this book look beautiful.

Then we'd like to say an extra thank you to all those who put their time in for free and therefore made this book possible:
STEPHEN, KEVIN and MAX, for your insights into the world of food and wine
MICHELLE, for your efficiency and organisation helping BEN in the kitchen
BECKY, for helping SIMON with the wine matches
CARLOS COELHO, for your support and technical expertise
And to those selfless recipe testers: ANA, BRETT, DANA, DEBORAH, EROL, ESTHER, GEORGINA, LUPI, MARTIN, NICI, NYKEETA and PRISCILLA

Finally, a massive thank you to all the Salt Yard Group staff, past and present, who have made the restaurants what they are.

RAMON OTTING's dramatic oil paintings of vineyards hang at Salt Yard and Opera Tavern. He produced the chapter introduction illustrations especially for the cookbook and is also offering them as limited edition prints.

PEDRO D'ALMEIDA is our barman at Dehesa and also a talented artist. We commissioned him to do the illustrations for the cover and endpapers. He is available for other private commissions.

To ask any questions regarding the artwork or to order prints from RAMON, please email info@saltyard.co.uk

Vintage Chart

Region

Italy

	1995	1996	1997	1998	1999	2000	2001
Barolo	★★★	★★★★★	★★★★★	★★★★	★★★★	★★★★★	★★★★
Barbaresco	★★★	★★★★★	★★★★★	★★★★	★★★★	★★★★★	★★★★
Friuli	★★★	★★★	★★★★	★★★★	★★★★	★★★★★	★★★
Amarone	★★★★★	★★	★★★★★	★★★★★	★★★★	★★★★★	★★★★
Alto Adige	★★★	★★★	★★★	★★	★★★	★★★★★	★★★
Chianti	★★★★★	★★★★	★★★★★	★★★★	★★★★★	★★★★	★★★★
Brunello	★★★★★	★★★	★★★★★	★★★★	★★★★	★★★	★★★
Bolgheri	★★★★	★★★★	★★★★	★★★★	★★★★	★★	★★★
Maremma	★★★★	★★★★	★★★★★	★★★★	★★★	★★★	★★★
Campania	★★★★	★★★	★★★★	★★★★	★★★★	★★★★★	★★★★
Umbria	★★★★	★★★	★★★★	★★★★★	★★★★	★★★★	★★★
Sardinia	★★★★	★★★★	★★★	★★★★	★★★★	★★★★	★★★★
Sicily	★★★★	★★★	★★★	★★★	★★	★★★	★★★

Spain

	1995	1996	1997	1998	1999	2000	2001
Rioja	★★★★★	★★★	★★★	★★★	★★★★	★★★	★★★★
Ribeiro de Duero	★★★★★	★★★★	★★★	★★★	★★★	★★★	★★★★
Galicia	☆	☆	★★★	★★★	★★★★	★★★	★★★★
Bierzo	★★★★★	★★★★	★★★	★★★	★★★	★★★★	★★★★
Toro	★★★★	★★★★	★★★	★★★★	★★★★★	★★★★★	★★★★
Somantano	★★★★★	★★★★	★★★	★★★★★	★★★★	★★★★	★★★★
Priorat	★★★★★	★★★★★	★★★	★★★★★	★★★★	★★★★	★★★★
Penedes	★★★★	★★★★	★★★★	★★★★★		★★★★	★★★★